D1606226

To
From
Date

ONE MINUTE Devotions FOR Mothers

365 DAILY MOMENTS *with* GOD

One Minute Devotions for Mothers: 365 Daily Moments with God

First Edition, March 2019

Published by:

P.O. Box 1010
Siloam Springs, AR 72761
dayspring.com

Key Contributors: Paige DeRuyscher, Kristin Morris, Anna Rendell, Amanda White, and Rachel Wojo

Designed and Typeset by: Greg Jackson of thinkpen.design

Printed in China
Prime: 89889
ISBN: 978-1-68408-617-7

JANUARY 1

Maybe it was as simple as getting all the clean laundry folded.

"If I can get this done, my heart will feel content."

Perhaps it was losing the baby weight or perfecting the meal plans.

No matter the goal, no one but you realizes that you didn't meet it. However, you carry the guilt. You mentally beat yourself up for not accomplishing what you set out to do.

Parenting doesn't come with a finish line; don't measure success by the checks on the to-do list. Our heavenly Father is simply looking for a heart like His—one that will focus on loving despite the laundry piles, folded or not.

But by the grace of God I am what I am, and His grace to me was not without effect.
I CORINTHIANS 15:10 NIV

JANUARY 2

Some days it's just hard to love. It's difficult to give to others the love we've been given. God understands and therefore provides the *grace lens*. It has the power to change our perspective, soften our view, and remove anything that keeps our hearts from seeing another's worth. Such love is full of grace and free of condition—and it's the truest way for us to reveal to others the *realness* of God.

Let us come boldly to the throne of our gracious God. There we will receive His mercy, and we will find grace to help us when we need it most.
HEBREWS 4:16 NLT

JANUARY 3

She was a mess, and the town knew it. Married and divorced four times. Living with another man. Not the most reputable neighbor. In fact, she was so shunned that the normal social activity for women in the town was an event she avoided every day. She went by herself to draw water when no one else was around.

When Jesus spoke, He changed her life. And she knew it. And when she, a normally edgy and reserved woman, went running through the streets with excitement, it was clear something had changed!

We will overcome by the blood of the Lamb and the word of our testimony (Revelation 12:11). So tell the world—just start with your neighbors—what God has done in your life. It may just make history.

From that city many of the Samaritans believed in Him because of the word of the woman who testified, "He told me all the things that I have done."
JOHN 4:39 NASB

JANUARY 4

God's love for us is strong. Nothing can ever separate us from God's love, and God asks us to love others, but not with any power of our own. We won't last long if we're relying on our own strength. But God will give us the strength we need, and that strength is only a prayer away.

When I pray, You answer me and encourage me by giving me the strength I need.
PSALM 138:3 TLB

JANUARY 5

There are days when we can't understand ourselves, let alone our children. We are intricate, complex beings by design, and that can make parenting frustrating! Although we think things that shock us (*Where did that come from?*), say things that disappoint us (*Did that really just come out of my mouth?*), and do things that confuse us (*Why in the world did I do that?*)—none of it catches God off guard. He is not surprised by our sins nor our shortcomings, but stands ready to redeem them. Whatever regrets you have in mothering, give them over to the Lord and put them in His care. He is prepared to handle them. Trust God to turn your regrets into a deeper relationship with Him and your children.

Thank You for making me so wonderfully complex! Your workmanship is marvelous—how well I know it.
PSALM 139:14 NLT

JANUARY 6

When you become a parent, it doesn't take long to learn that what you do and say are being watched. You soon encounter adorable moments where a toddler repeats "oh goodness!" or "okeydokey," or whatever you're apt to say in everyday life. You also learn quickly if you have a tendency to say or do things that are not appropriate for a two-year-old!

Children are wired to mimic and learn from the world around them. As children of God, so are we. That's why it's so important to look to the Lord for our example. If not, our default will be to learn from the world.

Who is watching you today? And where do you have your own eyes trained?

We love, because He first loved us.
I JOHN 4:19 NASB

JANUARY 7

Boundaries. We love them. We hate them. Sometimes we'd rather not deal with them. But one thing is true: we need them. And guess what? So did Jesus—God in the flesh, showing us how to live life to the full. Yes! He was surrounded by people in need. Yes! He poured out His life to serve. But He also "often withdrew" from the crowd to be alone and pray. He knew that answering "yes" to what the Father was calling Him into might mean saying "no" or "wait" to what was happening in the moment. Does this mean He didn't care? We know that's not true! It meant He knew what He needed in order to be refreshed—to connect with His Father and prepare for the journey ahead. Let's ask the Lord how we're being invited into that rhythm of rest today.

But Jesus often withdrew to lonely places and prayed.

LUKE 5:16 NIV

JANUARY 8

It can be so hard to wait. Never mind the waiting room, long lines of traffic, or a much anticipated letter in the mail. When the waiting we're doing is on God, it can seem like forever! And how do we handle it when the answer is one we didn't want? Well, think about this: an answer from God means that the God of the universe is in relationship with us! He cares enough to hear our hearts and respond. What a beautiful thing—God's no may be a no, but it still shows His closeness and love.

The mind of man plans his way, but
the LORD directs his steps.
PROVERBS 16:9 NASB

JANUARY 9

The situation couldn't be more chaotic! The dog just spilled his water, your toddler chose this moment to strip down to his diaper, Grandma's number buzzes your cell phone, and you're supposed to be ready for a date night with your husband—ten minutes ago!

In the heat of moments like these, your ability to make quick decisions is s-t-r-e-t-c-h-e-d.

"I just can't be everything to everyone all the time!" Anxiety looms large.

This is the time to cry to your heavenly Father for relief. He knows every circumstance and detail. He promises He will be with you any time of day, especially when you feel torn in different directions.

As for me, I call to God, and the LORD saves me. Evening, morning and noon I cry out in distress, and He hears my voice.

PSALM 55:16–17 NIV

JANUARY 10

Our kindness is a little drop of God's love in the world—and by His power and grace, a little goes a long way! Someone's day can be changed by your kind words or actions. A person who hasn't felt loved in a while can be reminded that God sees them...and hasn't left them. Someone else might need a bright spot in the day to have the courage to go on. God knows the need—and uses us to bring the love!

How kind the Lord is! How good He is!
PSALM 116:5 NLT

JANUARY 11

Kids today know a lot. But there are some things kids just don't know—like how long it takes to wrap presents the night before Christmas, or about leaving work early so they don't have to ride the bus, or how packing lunches every day for twelve years can get old. Motherhood is full of hard jobs and mundane tasks that can make you feel very unseen and unknown. Hagar, a mother in the Bible, felt so unappreciated by her family she ran away to the desert. (Whoa. Don't you feel better about your day now?) While she was there, God spoke to her and gave her a hopeful promise for her future. In turn, Hagar called God "the One who sees me." For those days you feel alone, unappreciated, and unseen, remember the One who sees you every minute of the day—our God!

She gave this name to the LORD who spoke to her: "You are the God who sees me," for she said, "I have now seen the One who sees me."
GENESIS 16:13 NIV

JANUARY 12

Everything we do with a spirit of love makes God smile. After all, love changes hearts, and in the moment God's love is shared, people get a glimpse of *Him*. He's the source of every good thing in our lives, and His love is the greatest thing we'll ever give *or* receive. Remembering that God's love enables us to shine, consider what you might do to keep your life lighting the way to Him.

God doesn't miss anything. He knows perfectly well all the love you've shown...and that you keep at it.
HEBREWS 6:10 THE MESSAGE

JANUARY 13

With every stage of parenting comes a unique set of challenges. Just when you think you have it figured out, everything changes! It's sort of like an obstacle course…running a race with new challenges around every bend. You're prepared, but you're not prepared. You've been in training but not for this. You're tired, but you can't take a break. The physical, mental, and emotional exhaustion of caring for your children is making you doubt your ability to finish well. How do you endure the marathon of parenting? Focus on Jesus, the source of your strength. Ask Him to equip you first thing in the morning, receive what He offers you throughout the day, and thank Him before you go to bed at night. He has everything you need.

Let us run with endurance the race God has set before us. We do this by keeping our eyes on Jesus, the champion who initiates and perfects our faith.

HEBREWS 12:1–2 NLT

JANUARY 14

Take a close look at today's Scripture. Let it really sink in. Breathe in the truth of it: God considers you family. Not your loopy Aunt Sally who talks too much and kisses too hard. Not the brother you no longer speak to because of that thing you fought over twenty years ago. The Lord, our God, loves you as family He wants to be with. He decided you should exist, and He created you. Then He called you by name and placed you right where you belong. Earthly family is full of strange, wonderful human dynamics. But with God it's pretty straightforward: you're loved beyond measure.

He who sanctifies and those who are sanctified all have one source. That is why he is not ashamed to call them brothers.
HEBREWS 2:11 ESV

JANUARY 15

If you've ever been skiing, you've probably seen a color-coded map of the mountain. For a newbie, the green trail means "Go;" blue means "Maybe later;" and black means "Don't even think about it!" But once a skier has a few runs under her belt, she has a choice: keep taking the easy route or venture into the unknown.

Our lives are like that—always offering the comfort of the familiar or the opportunity to step into something new. And it seems that wherever God is working, there's a call into newness, to step out, rise up, trust more deeply, and live more fully. It's always our choice, and it doesn't change His love for us. But when we do sacrifice our comfort zones, we'll often find that what we gain is far greater than we could've imagined.

"Come," He said. Then Peter got down out of the boat, walked on the water and came toward Jesus.
MATTHEW 14:29 NIV

JANUARY 16

If only we could see into the future. Far into the future, into the heavens, into eternity. If we could understand what eternal life with the Lord will be like, we probably wouldn't think twice about the things that worry us today. The fast food meal we crave would taste like dust compared to the table set before us. The movie with the questionable rating wouldn't even get our second glance. The things of heaven can't truly be imagined, planned for, or measured. But we can dream. And thank Him in advance for choosing us as His heavenly kids.

Blessed be the God and Father of our Lord Jesus Christ, who has blessed us with every spiritual blessing in the heavenly places in Christ.
EPHESIANS 1:3 NASB

JANUARY 17

A friend texts you asking for advice about how to mold the future of her soon-to-be graduate. As if you have all the answers yourself! Worry has threatened to rule your thoughts as you begin the mental process of launching your child into independent living. Frets about the state of society whip around in your mind. *Our culture can be such a cruel place. What if he forgets to track his spending? Did we miss an application deadline?*

Helping your child move into a new season can be scary for you, Mama. But it doesn't have to be. God has promised that His plan for His children is more than we can comprehend. No matter the next step, He's still in control.

The Lord will fulfill his purpose for me; your steadfast love, O Lord, endures forever.
PSALM 138:8 ESV

JANUARY 18

There's no mountain too high that the Lord can't see over it. No ocean too deep that He can't cross it to reach you. No desert too dry that He can't rain down His love and mercy. God will stop at nothing to love you. He spares no expense for His children. We can slow Him down with our disbelief, or miss His tenderness if we keep our hearts hard. But stay soft and pliable, trust Him with your needs, and He'll surprise you. God has all power at His fingertips. But it's you He wants above all else.

Thus says God the LORD, who created the heavens and stretched them out, who spread out the earth and its offspring, who gives breath to the people on it and spirit to those who walk in it, "I am the LORD."

ISAIAH 42:5–6 NASB

JANUARY 19

"Pinterest-perfect" has become a real word. Maybe not in the dictionary, but everyone knows what it means. It's the mama who has a Chip-and-Jo–worthy home, a doting husband, splendid birthday parties for her kids, paleo-gluten-free-dairy-free nutritious masterpieces for dinner, and still has cute hair and clothes as she happily cleans her shower with a toothbrush.It's a good thing Jesus doesn't demand perfection from us. When a sinful woman came to Him and poured oil on His feet (hello waste! hello expensive! hello super weird and embarrassing!), He demanded, "Leave her alone... she did what she could!" Jesus knows our limits, our weaknesses, and yes, our sin. His desire is for us to just be in relationship with Him. He sends our accusers (even if they are only a nice Pinterest board) away with a word and embraces the small things we can do for Him as a beautiful gift!

"Leave her alone," said Jesus. "Why are you bothering her? She has done a beautiful thing to Me. The poor you will always have with you, and you can help them any time you want. But you will not always have Me. She did what she could."

MARK 14:6–8 NIV

JANUARY 20

One of the best ways to teach our children is by example. From the moment they are born, they are listening to what we say and watching what we do. They are learning from our words and our actions, whether we are trying to teach them anything or not. They form opinions and habits based on their observations of us and their experiences with us. Regardless of the words we speak, the loudest voice we have for teaching them is the way we live our everyday lives. This is especially true when it comes to relationships. What is your behavior teaching your children about how to treat others? Are you showing relational integrity with the people in your own home? You won't always walk it out perfectly, and neither will they. But when your choices in both word and deed honor God first, those around you will also be honored.

We are careful to be honorable before the Lord, but we also want everyone else to see that we are honorable.
II CORINTHIANS 8:21 NLT

JANUARY 21

It's so encouraging to get a surprise text, phone call, card, or letter, because they all send the same spirit-lifting message: someone is thinking about me! Now ponder the truth that God thinks about you *constantly*. What is it that initiates His moment-by-moment awareness of you? Love. He loves you so much that He can't—and won't—take His mind off of you. You're far too valuable to Him to neglect, *any* time of *any* day.

How precious it is, Lord, to realize that You are thinking about me constantly!
PSALM 139:17 TLB

JANUARY 22

Kids and chores: not always a pleasant combination. Ever hear a little grumbling? See a few eye rolls? Find yourself wishing they'd just lighten up and finish up already? Their attitudes can hold up a mirror for us: *What comes from our own hearts and mouths when we're working?*

In our homes, our offices, volunteering at church or school. Does our presence feel like sunshine or more like a rain cloud rolling in? Sure we're not going to love every mundane task set before us, but we are *always* free to choose gratitude over grumbling. We're free to find joy— if not in the work we're doing then in the One we're ultimately doing it for. We may preach this to our kids time and again, but our actions will always speak louder than words.

Whatever you do, work at it with all your heart, as working for the Lord.
COLOSSIANS 3:23 NIV

JANUARY 23

The right things you do today can only come from a heart transformed by pure love. When we realize the helplessness of our human capabilities and the power of God's perfect love to influence our actions, lives are touched and changed for good. Smiles, words, a hug, a helping hand—keep your eyes open for moments to do what's right, and be ready to receive the blessing of joy.

And so the Lord has paid me with His blessings, for I have done what is right, and I am pure of heart.
PSALM 18:24 TLB

JANUARY 24

You knew before you woke up this morning that the day would be challenging. One child has an eye appointment and the other a music lesson. Your boss called to say she was running late and could you meet with her client? The feeling of being needed by so many people at once begins to feel less like an honor and more like a demand. How can you possibly be everywhere at the same time? You can't. But God sees you and knows the details. He promises to meet all the needs. He will use you as He sees fit; rest in Him today.

My God will meet all your needs according to the riches of His glory in Christ Jesus.
PHILIPPIANS 4:19 NIV

JANUARY 25

God loves you in every season,
yet His love is not seasonal;
He loves you in every circumstance,
yet His love is not circumstantial;
He loves you in every condition,
yet His love is not conditional.
ROY LESSIN

Jesus Christ is the same yesterday
and today and forever.
HEBREWS 13:8 ESV

JANUARY 26

Have you ever wanted to do more for the Lord? Maybe start a ministry or volunteer for one? Or write or speak to encourage other women and members of the church? Sometimes doing seems like the thing God wants most. It's easy to assume that if we love God, doing more-and-better for Him is the ultimate plan. When Jesus spoke to Peter after the resurrection, He told Peter to "feed His lambs" (yes, the little babies!). He would later tell Peter and the disciples to go into all the world and preach the gospel, but His first directive to Peter was to just feed the children. Feed them with God's Word, with His love and promises. What a weight off for a mama! Don't let the Super Important Spiritual To-Do List weigh you down. Just feed the little lambs in front of you. Jesus sees that as true love.

When they had finished eating, Jesus said to Simon Peter, "Simon son of John, do you love Me more than these?" "Yes, Lord," he said, "you know that I love You." Jesus said, "Feed my lambs."

JOHN 21:15 NIV

JANUARY 27

Pressure has been mounting at work and all the training in the world doesn't seem to be helping you keep your head on straight. You forgot the milk at the grocery store last night, even though it was first on the list. You're not alone; even the most educated can feel scatterbrained at times! If feeling distracted seems to be commonplace for you, God's Word says He will help you. His guidance is ever available. What if you paused to remind yourself of His promise to provide wisdom and leadership?

I instruct you in the way of wisdom
and lead you along straight paths.
PROVERBS 4:11 NIV

JANUARY 28

Don't you wish you had all the answers to every phase of mothering you'll ever be faced with? We've all been there...aching for our children...at a total loss for what to say or do to make it all better. Whether we have a newborn who won't stop crying, a toddler who has spent the majority of the day telling us no, a child who is being bullied at school, an adolescent who is struggling with their identity, or a teen who is navigating a difficult relationship, here is the ongoing truth of motherhood: we need wisdom. How many times have we cried (literally) while crying out to God in desperation, "Help me!" The good news is that our prayers do not come as a surprise to Him. He is waiting for us to ask and prepared to give us an answer. We need only to keep asking and keep listening.

Tune your ears to wisdom, and concentrate on understanding. Cry out for insight, and ask for understanding. Search for them as you would for silver; seek them like hidden treasures.

PROVERBS 2:2–4 NLT

JANUARY 29

In life there are moments of joy, moments of sorrow, and moments of crying out for rhyme and reason. Always and without fail we get God's presence, but oftentimes we wait to see His purpose. The great news? Strength gets bigger while we wait. Our lives become larger to make room for trust, faith, hope, and peace. That's the kind of stuff we want to be blessed with, because it makes every other blessing even better.

The moment I called out, You stepped in;
You made my life large with strength.
PSALM 138:3 THE MESSAGE

JANUARY 30

"It's nothing compared to what you're going through." How often have words like these come out of our mouths? Maybe we're telling a friend about a struggle we're going through when we suddenly remember her recent prayer request. We think: How can I be whining about my little issue? It's nothing compared to that!

Before we go dismissing ourselves, let's remember it all matters to our Father. Yes! We are called to support and encourage others. But we're not called to compare our hurts or dismiss our own tough times. We can love our neighbor well—perhaps even more authentically—when we allow space and grace for ourselves. The Lord's compassion is for all of us, always. And the more we receive in our own time of need, the more we can pour out to others in theirs.

The Lord is good to all; He has compassion on all He has made.
PSALM 145:9 NIV

JANUARY 31

God's timing isn't always easy to understand, but it's always perfect. The time between our circumstance and His answer is a period of hope and trust. There are seasons when God asks us to trust Him wholeheartedly without seeing where we're going or knowing how we're growing. We can be sure that *everything* we face is filtered through God's hand—and He'll use it to make our hearts like His.

There is a right time for everything.
ECCLESIASTES 3:1 TLB

FEBRUARY 1

She heads out the door with the car keys for the first time. The smile on her face is imprinted on your mind and you tuck the memory into your heart, all the while praying for her safety. Praying for your child's needs can be scary, especially in today's world. Should you pray for safety first or last? Or both? Physical needs are important. But emotional needs are too. Then there's the desire for healthy friendships and a personal relationship with God. No matter the order of the words you pray or even if you're feeling like you have no words, be assured that God knows your heart for your child. The Spirit covers for you when you just don't know what to pray.

In the same way, the Spirit helps us in our weakness. We do not know what we ought to pray for, but the Spirit Himself intercedes for us through wordless groans.

ROMANS 8:26 NIV

FEBRUARY 2

The depth of God's grace will always surpass the depth of our weaknesses. In truth, His grace has no measure. It's deeper than our deepest need and able to sustain us in moments when we feel too weak to fight a moment longer. His grace covers you, His strength carries you—and the more you lean in, the more you'll stand strong.

My grace is sufficient for you, for My strength is made perfect in weakness.
II CORINTHIANS 12:9 NKJV

FEBRUARY 3

If only you could find the energy. Whether it's been illness or fatigue, spiritual or physical, you've been digging deep and coming up empty. It's easy to run out of steam if you forget that God is your strength. His very breath began yours and continues to provide each filling of your lungs. His strength moves mountains and it can surely move your body. You are His masterpiece and He delights in propelling you forward. He is the essence of your ability to live, move, and be. Ask Him for the power to keep going.

For in Him we live and move and have our being.
ACTS 17:28 NIV

FEBRUARY 4

It seems unnecessary to pour out our heart to God. After all, "The Lord sees every heart and knows every plan and thought" (I Chronicles 28:9 NLT). The pouring out isn't for Him; it's for us. Confessing our need helps us realize our need for Him. We can't handle our days with a closed-door policy on our hearts. We have to pour out everything—from pressures to praise—because when we let weaknesses out, His strength comes in.

Trust in Him at all times. Pour out your heart to Him, for God is our refuge.
PSALM 62:8 NLT

FEBRUARY 5

Fingernails on a chalkboard. Cracking knuckles. Open mouth chewing. Always-barking dogs. Junk mail. Slow Internet. What is it that pushes you over the edge? What's the super annoying thing that just makes you lose it? Maybe it's something serious—like the way your kid reacts to discipline or your husband unknowingly slights you. Whatever it is that steals your peace, it can feel like careening down a giant ravine engulfing you and your good attitude. God promises that when we love His Word, we will have peace and nothing—not close-talkers, crying babies, or unmade beds—will make us stumble. Try penciling in fifteen minutes with Father God and His Word tomorrow; you'll feel His peace envelop and protect you instead!

Great peace have those who love your law,
and nothing can make them stumble.
PSALM 119:165 NIV

FEBRUARY 6

All day, every day, God's love and goodness are coming at you. *Pursuing* you. Where you are, He *is*...with good plans, good-for-you experiences, and good-for-your-heart opportunities to grow. Even when days feel hard and leave questions, you're standing smack-dab in the middle of the love that's working everything together for something really, really good.

Your goodness and unfailing love will
pursue me all the days of my life.
PSALM 23:6 NLT

FEBRUARY 7

What had happened between them was years ago, but it had formed a deep rift between the once-friends. For years the two of them struggled to serve together in their ministry. But things finally crumbled beyond repair...at least beyond repair by the world's standards.

Instead of giving up, the women met a year after they had separated. They opened up about the hard things, shed a few tears, and showed one another the grace God had given them. They tried again. And this time, they experienced the restoration of the Spirit.

Every effort means never giving up on the people in your life. Even if it takes years and is full of mistakes. Leaving room for the Holy Spirit to do amazing things is never wasted time.

With all humility and gentleness, with patience, showing tolerance for one another in love, being diligent to preserve the unity of the Spirit in the bond of peace.

EPHESIANS 4:2–3 NASB

FEBRUARY 8

Even on days when your mind is cluttered with fear and worry, love will make its way in. It will find the smallest clearing and have the biggest presence. Kick the cares aside and focus on it. God is right in front of you, that monumental love reaching out to hold you close and whisper, "Let Me have them. Every worry, every fear. I've got them—and I've got you."

Nothing can ever separate us from His love…our fears for today, our worries about tomorrow….
ROMANS 8:38 TLB

FEBRUARY 9

"I picked these for you, Mom!" When tiny hands reach up, carefully grasping a little bunch of weeds they've gathered, they might as well be holding a dozen roses. Gifts from our children warm our hearts like nothing else. And the same is true of our heavenly Father's heart toward us. He delights in our giving, no matter what the gift. He's not waiting for the most impressive act or the biggest sacrifice. He doesn't compare our little bouquet of dandelions with the next person's. He sees our intentions and simply smiles on our desire to be generous—just as we cherish the loving efforts of our own children. Even the smallest act of kindness is precious to Him.

Do not forget to do good and to share,
for with such sacrifices God is well pleased.
HEBREWS 13:16 NKJV

FEBRUARY 10

First pray, then do. Four tiny words that change the course of a day. Can you imagine following the admonishment in this Scripture without fail? Don't worry…pray. God knew we couldn't do both at the same time, so He gave us the best and only way to defeat worry moment by moment: "Talk to Me about it."

Don't worry about anything;
instead, pray about everything.
PHILIPPIANS 4:6 TLB

FEBRUARY 11

Sometimes you wonder if he'll ever understand the beauty of mutual respect. Your child's attitude has worn you down. You've cried. You've pleaded. You've begged. You've punished. You've read every Christian parenting book on strong-willed behaviors that you could get your hands on. But ultimately, you long to pray for him more than ever. You've got this. God has equipped you with the power of prayer! Praying for your child is the most influential parenting action you can take. The God who spoke light into the darkness is still shining His light in and through hearts today.

For God, who said, "Let light shine out of darkness," has shone in our hearts to give the light of the knowledge of the glory of God in the face of Jesus Christ.
II CORINTHIANS 4:6 ESV

FEBRUARY 12

It's most likely that if you are in need of groceries, you get in the car and head to the nearest Walmart, Aldi, or Safeway. If you want to see a movie, you either turn on Netflix or look up a new release at the local theater.

It makes good sense that when we need hope, we go to the source of all hope. Hope is God's specialty. He invented it. When things looked bleak, Jesus came along bearing all the possibility of freedom and eternal life. And it didn't end at the cross. Hope is a necessary part of life. It fills and sustains us. And we're meant to share it with the world around us. So go to the source today and get you some hope!

Now may the God of hope fill you with all joy and peace in believing, so that you will abound in hope by the power of the Holy Spirit.
ROMANS 15:13 NASB

FEBRUARY 13

Sometimes the schedules, events, practices, recitals, games, field trips, and all the things that come with being a mom get so overwhelming that it's easy to forget about the most important part—mothering! Remember when Martha and Mary had Jesus over to their house? Mary sat at Jesus's feet while Martha bustled around the house. When Martha complained to Jesus that all the things were not going to be accomplished on time, He basically told her to chill out. He stated that Mary had chosen the one truly important activity on the schedule.

Today, I want to put aside the list and put the One Necessary Thing, rather the One Necessary Person— Jesus—in my view. I want to put the anxiety and trouble and distraction away and focus on what Jesus has for me as a wife, mom, and believer.

But the Lord answered her, "Martha, Martha, you are anxious and troubled about many things, but one thing is necessary. Mary has chosen the good portion, which will not be taken away from her."

LUKE 10:41–42 ESV

FEBRUARY 14

Two sisters were taken to Disneyland by their parents. The older girl worried about the rides. Would she get sick? She worried about being away from home. Would the dog miss them too much? Would the airplane ride be scary?

The younger girl imagined it would be wonderful. She thought of the characters, balloons, treats, and fun rides. She thought of the stories she'd have to tell when she got back. Mostly she thought about the unknown possibilities.

Who do you think had more fun? Worry is a life-stealer, a fun-thief. God tells us not to worry, because there's no good that comes from it. All the good comes from living expectantly for our amazing God to be His amazing self.

Who of you by being worried can
add a single hour to his life?
MATTHEW 6:27 NASB

FEBRUARY 15

Conflict is inevitable in a home full of unique, imperfect people. Personalities are different, preferences are different, and sometimes it's just a matter of "That's not fair!" When people disagree, conversations can heat up quickly, and anger is as close as the very next word. How does God call us to engage with those we don't understand or strongly disagree with? It's our natural response in the flesh to engage in conflict as flamethrowers, carelessly firing emotion-driven words to make sure we are heard, get our point across, or prove that we are right. But God calls us to respond as extinguishers, carefully putting out the embers of anger with Spirit-driven conduct. The next time tempers flare in your family—because they will—take the gentle way out. Be extra thoughtful about your words and your tone, making sure they reflect the One who is living within you.

A gentle answer turns away wrath,
but a harsh word stirs up anger.
PROVERBS 15:1 NIV

FEBRUARY 16

In this demanding and distracting world, rest is so important. But many people aren't sure how to rest in a way that fills and refreshes them. Resting in Jesus isn't too unlike resting on a beach or in a hammock, with a cool glass of water and a good book in hand. Your mind releases its worries—to Jesus. Your body relaxes, as if wrapped in strong arms. Your thoughts turn to all the good qualities of the One who loves you more than anything. Resting in Jesus can happen at the office or at home, in nature or on a busy street. Try taking five minutes today and deliberately practicing the art of resting in Jesus.

Come to Me, all who are weary and heavy-laden, and I will give you rest.
MATTHEW 11:28 NASB

FEBRUARY 17

Life with kids can feel like a science experiment. This thing doesn't work, so we try that thing. A new chore chart seems helpful; let's stick with it! Oops. Definitely not playing that sport again…and so on. There are so many pieces and parts, choices and changes, and voices out there shouting, "Do this, buy this, make this…and all will be well!" But life in Christ offers a simpler way. We don't have to scramble for the right, better, new, and improved everything. We don't have to stumble around in the dark when the Light of the world lives within us. We can lay it all out before Him and simply ask for guidance. Then pay close attention to His leading in the days that follow. Remember: He cares about the big things, the small things, and everything in between.

Whether you turn to the right or to the left, your ears will hear a voice behind you, saying, "This is the way; walk in it."
ISAIAH 30:21 NIV

FEBRUARY 18

You're contagious! Did you know? But in the very best way. Every time you encourage someone. Every time you let someone cut in line in front of you. Every time you make a decision based on whatever is true, right, noble, lovely, pure, excellent, or praiseworthy (Philippians 4:8)...the goodness of God is poured out. Of course, it works the other way too. Negative words and actions can have an effect on those around us. It can be a challenge to live out the love of Jesus when circumstances are testing our emotions and patience. But every time we choose love, everyone wins.

In speech, conduct, love, faith and purity, show yourself an example of those who believe.
I TIMOTHY 4:12 NASB

FEBRUARY 19

Choosing your attitude is as deliberate as choosing your outfit. How are you going to go about your day? Will you put on a veil of pessimism and entitlement? Or will you choose to wear kindness and encouragement? Will you hope for the best, or expect the worst?

Just as it takes deliberate effort to put pants and a top on, it takes effort to wear the virtues given us by God. Especially in the face of challenges. But consider it an honor. Like wearing a uniform to a job you love, it's a privilege to have His grace and mercy at our fingertips.

So, as those who have been chosen of God, holy and beloved, put on a heart of compassion, kindness, humility, gentleness and patience.... Beyond all these things put on love, which is the perfect bond of unity.

COLOSSIANS 3:12, 14 NASB

FEBRUARY 20

In a race, there can be only one first-place winner. But in the kingdom, winning is about finishing well. What does that mean? It means devoting our lives to loving the Lord our God with all our heart, soul, mind, and strength and loving others as ourselves. It means serving others with a heart like Jesus. Living like this, you can be sure that the prize is within your reach. So stay strong, press on, and keep believing. You've got what it takes to be a kingdom-class athlete. Train hard and follow Coach Holy Spirit's instructions. You may just have a medal coming!

I press on toward the goal for the prize of the upward call of God in Christ Jesus.
PHILIPPIANS 3:14 NASB

FEBRUARY 21

Open mouth. Insert foot. We've all done it, sometimes even clapping a hand over our mouths because we can't believe the words that flew out. Words can harm hearts. Words can wound souls. Words can spew like sewage. God tells us to not let any unwholesome talk come out of our mouth. (Not any?!) He tells us to use our words to build others up. When we look at our kids, what words would build up their little hearts? What words would lay a foundation of life and peace? The words we speak can actually benefit those who listen. When our words are well-crafted and well-chosen, our children and others around us will be built up to do more for others and for God's kingdom!

Do not let any unwholesome talk come out of your mouths, but only what is helpful for building others up according to their needs, that it may benefit those who listen.

EPHESIANS 4:29 NIV

FEBRUARY 22

Tuck yourself into the arms of the Father, and you'll never be alone. Not in the worst of times. Not when the job ends and the bills are due. Not when he comes home late—again. Or when she still can't seem to stop drinking. You'll be cared for richly. Your roots will go down deep into His love and stay there. And as you learn, you'll grow. God will take care of every one of your needs. Not only will you survive the drought, but you will truly thrive. You'll become an example for the world, a light, a bright spot that people look to. And that's when you can point to Jesus.

The LORD will continually guide you, and satisfy your desire in scorched places, and give strength to your bones; and you will be like a watered garden, and like a spring of water whose waters do not fail.

ISAIAH 58:11 NASB

FEBRUARY 23

It's probably safe to say that in every mother's nature is the tendency to worry about her children. We worry about small things and big things—anything and everything that could affect our children's well-being. We stress over sickness and sport teams, safety and satisfaction, soulmates and sin. Our fears are significantly heightened when we have no control over or visibility to the outcome. But there is Someone who has all control and all visibility, and we can talk directly to Him about our every concern.

Today, practice turning your worry into a warrior's cry, and fight for your children in prayer. May it become a daily practice to trade your worry for trust, and may you experience the peace that passes all understanding, knowing that you have placed your children's every need into the able and loving hands of the Lord.

Don't worry about anything; instead, pray about everything. Tell God what you need, and thank Him for all He has done. Then you will experience God's peace, which exceeds anything we can understand.

PHILIPPIANS 4:6–7 NLT

FEBRUARY 24

Have you ever found yourself pressed beyond your limits? Marathoners experience that at the beginning of a training season. They might wonder, after their first 3-mile run, how they will ever go 26.2 miles without stopping. But eventually they do! Those who grieve the loss of a loved one know about limits. There are times when "enough is enough" crosses the mind. But they still keep going through the process of pain and healing.

Grace is a miraculous thing. God provides grace for the moment, right when we need it—rarely too early and never too late. And it always lasts as long as we need. The experience of spiritual stamina isn't always easy or fun. But to know His grace in the process can be very rewarding.

Those who wait for the LORD will gain new strength; they will mount up with wings like eagles, they will run and not get tired, they will walk and not become weary.
ISAIAH 40:31 NASB

FEBRUARY 25

How often do we compare ourselves to others? Maybe it's physically (*How does she stay in such good shape?*). Or emotionally (*Why can't I get my kids to listen like that mom?*). And what about spiritual comparison? That can be the worst! (*I should be volunteering for VBS and making time for that family devotional and waking up early for prayer...*) We may admire the ways others live their faith and feel the need to add on to our already-heaping pile of expectations. But let's remember that in Christ, we each become a one-of-a-kind expression of God's Spirit. We each have our own mix of gifts, circumstances, and seasons of life. We don't need some recipe for spiritual perfection. We just need Jesus. Let's ask Him to help us find joy in our own, unique journey today.

Show me the way I should go,
for to You I entrust my life.
PSALM 143:8 NIV

FEBRUARY 26

Even the closest of relationships go through the rockiest of times. And it's in moments like these that we desperately need the truth of God's brand of love. It's a love that just won't quit. His love is full of mercy, forgiveness, and hope. It helps erase the pain and build the future. Thankfully, God promises to give us what we need. And He cares very, very deeply about relationships. If you are in need of some healing love, just ask Him. Then wait and watch. You can believe for miraculous things.

Love...bears all things, believes all things, hopes all things, endures all things. Love never fails.
I CORINTHIANS 13:4, 7–8 NASB

FEBRUARY 27

Doctor's appointments, after-school activities, church ministry meetings, and the list continues to grow. While you stare at your planner, another text pops up with one more request. Then you pray, "Lord, how can I prioritize my time well?"

Scheduling can be such a tricky thing to balance. Maybe you've prayed over daily routines and labored over the calendar, but still your heart feels conflicted. You're unsure about whether you chose God's best plan. His Word reminds you that when you are seeking the Lord first, everything else will be taken care of. Seek Him first and He will add everything else into your schedule according to His promises.

But seek first His kingdom and His righteousness, and all these things will be given to you as well.
MATTHEW 6:33 NIV

FEBRUARY 28

Your checkbook had a great big red number on the balance line. No way to pay it back; the debt was just too big. And you couldn't help it. Just the luck of the draw.

And then came a billionaire with a ridiculous proposition: "I already paid it all. I gave you a fresh start and a full bank account to access at any time."

Now the choice is up to you. Do you withdraw from that account? Or are you so skeptical that you don't even go to the bank to see if what the billionaire said is true?

Jesus has done the paying. We get to receive, if we're willing. And we get to share the awesome news of debts paid off to anyone who will listen.

For the wages of sin is death, but the free gift of God is eternal life in Christ Jesus our Lord.
ROMANS 6:23 NASB

MARCH 1

Melancholy and sadness can be like a pebble kicked along a hill that keeps hopping, rolling, and skittering away, bouncing from one ledge and crevice to another until it rolls all the way to the bottom of a ravine. One trial, be it big or small, one trouble that overwhelms you for a minute can turn into a day, and glass-half-empty becomes the norm for you. When you feel that dip in your emotions, turn to the Lord and ask Him to teach you to party. Yes, party! King David tells us in one of his famous psalms that in God's presence there is "total celebration." Imagine being in the midst of the darkest times but turning to walk into God's bear hug and experiencing total celebration. This is the beautiful plan He has for you in His right hand!

You reveal the path of life to me; in Your presence is abundant joy; in Your right hand are eternal pleasures.

PSALM 16:11 HCSB

MARCH 2

You have gifts from the greatest Giver—and they're given to you to do the greatest amount of good. Today there will be moments to engage the special things God wove into you as an individual. He designed you to carry His gifts to the places and people on the path of your purpose. And your steps will leave a trail of joy, smiles, encouragement, hope, love, and strength.

Christ has given each of us special abilities—whatever He wants us to have out of His rich storehouse of gifts.
EPHESIANS 4:7 TLB

MARCH 3

Enemies study their prey, looking for signs that give away their weaknesses. Do you know your own weaknesses? Do you know your children's weaknesses? Not just the gaping obvious ones but the ones that look like hairline cracks? As believers, we have an enemy who is actively looking for vulnerabilities in our faith and is prepared to pounce at the first sign of weakness. How can we fight against the devil's schemes? Put on the full armor of God. Get dressed with every piece of armor meant for defending yourself, and ready yourself with the only piece of armor meant for attack—the sword of the Spirit, which is the Word of God. Scripture is how we fight. When you take the time to read it, memorize it, and recite it, you are preparing yourself for battle first. Then, you can teach your children how to fight for themselves.

Put on the full armor of God, so that you can take your stand against the devil's schemes.
EPHESIANS 6:11 NIV

MARCH 4

Grace is the beautiful reminder that God understands, forgives, and loves us—no matter what. Hold your head high today and keep going. Decide to be full of the joy of the Lord so you can be full of His mighty, glorious strength. Face the day and fill the moments with bravery and boldness, because God's got you in His arms of grace.

Be filled with His mighty, glorious strength so that you can keep going no matter what happens—always full of the joy of the Lord.
COLOSSIANS 1:11 TLB

MARCH 5

Here's a tough question to ask ourselves: *Is there anyone in my life I intentionally avoid?* Maybe it's someone who talks a lot or has a negative vibe. Maybe a neighbor kid or a coworker with a thousand questions. Some connections can be draining, and we need healthy boundaries to help us care for our hearts and use our time wisely. But it's also vital to remember that there are no chance meetings. All our circumstances unfold under the umbrella of God's loving care. When we do encounter someone we'd rather walk past, it's good to pause and ask the Holy Spirit to lead us. Trust Him to guide the conversation, to guard our hearts from negativity and bless our words with grace and truth. He's able to make our connections meaningful (even enjoyable!) and give us a way to move on when it's time.

My times are in Your hands.

PSALM 31:15 NIV

MARCH 6

All is well because you are loved. You are loved because you are priceless to God. No matter what happens in the moments of your day, His love for you is why you can hold your head high and believe that everything is going to be okay. Good things will be sweeter, tough things will be easier, mistakes will be forgiven—and the sun will set with Him loving you as unconditionally as ever.

We are able to hold our heads high no matter what happens and know that all is well, for we know how dearly God loves us.
ROMANS 5:5 TLB

MARCH 7

It's a new day. Whether the first day on a job or first week living in a new home, things are different. You're not sure if you really wanted this change, but it happened. Life is full of transitions, isn't it? The hardest part of transition is simply not knowing. Feeling like you can't predict the new normal strikes fear into your heart. When feeling uncomfortable in your routine causes you to be afraid, rest in God's promise to always be with you. Change does not need to produce fear. He will provide the courage to face any new situation!

Have I not commanded you? Be strong and courageous. Do not be afraid; do not be discouraged, for the LORD Your God will be with you wherever you go.

JOSHUA 1:9 NIV

MARCH 8

Nothing on this earth can stop God's love from reaching us when we need to see and feel it most...and thankfully, nothing will keep Him from showing it. He knows when we're at the end of our hope rope. Words, perfectly spoken or written; an out-of-the-blue act of kindness; the spotting of a favorite bird or the sun peeking through on a dreary day—they're little love notes saying, "I love you and I'm here."

Nothing can ever separate us from God's love.
ROMANS 8:38 NLT

MARCH 9

When kids first learn to walk, there's a lot of hand holding. Even when they are adept at every step, when we're walking through a crowd or over rough ground, mamas always have their little ones' hands tight in their own. As they get older, there's not as much hand holding as there are instructions to follow and stay close. One day those same kiddos will be driving to school by themselves! This same pattern is true in every area of our children's lives—we equip our kids with lessons, morals, and strategies to journey through life. We walk with them, at first almost doing it for them, then moving just a handsbreadth away, leading them down the right paths and over the big hazards. Soon they will be able to navigate more and more on their own. Let's pray God would help us lead our kids to Him!

Direct your children onto the right path, and when they are older, they will not leave it.
PROVERBS 22:6 NLT

MARCH 10

There's trust in stepping forward without fear. Our lives are a series of decisions to step in one direction or another. At times we won't see the path ahead. The sweet assurance we have is that God will keep us from slipping. If He has to widen the steps beneath our feet or catch us when we fall, He will.

You have made wide steps for my feet,
to keep them from slipping.
II SAMUEL 22:37 TLB

MARCH 11

God loves perfectly, and hallelujah for that! As mothers, as wives, as daughters, as sisters, as friends, and even as Christians, we fall crazy short in expressing love the way God defines it. We are far from being perfectly patient and perfectly kind. The love in our hearts is not always conveyed without envy or boasting or pride. We can be rude, selfish, and short-fused, while unknowingly finding ourselves playing tit for tat. How desperate we are to do better, yet how grateful are we that God's perfect love fills in the gaps where our imperfect love is lacking? Before you go to bed tonight, meditate on I Corinthians 13:4–7. Ask God to fill you with His love to overflowing so you can wake up tomorrow ready to pour it out to those around you. Let His perfect love be the theme of a new day in Christ!

Love is patient, love is kind.
Love does not envy,
is not boastful, is not conceited,
does not act improperly,
is not selfish, is not provoked,
and does not keep a record of wrongs.
I CORINTHIANS 13:4–5 HCSB

MARCH 12

God's plans for you are as special as you are. They were thoughtfully designed to align with your unique and wonderful wiring. But be sure that they're going to be about spreading the love. The one thing all God's plans have in common? They're good—good for pointing hearts to Him. His plans for each of us come down to that one thing, repeated in the moments that make up the days: love, love, love.

For I know the plans I have for you, says the Lord. They are plans for good and not for evil, to give you a future and a hope.
JEREMIAH 29:11 TLB

MARCH 13

Calendars. Sometimes it feels like they're running our lives. Every month, we open them to rows of empty squares. And soon, appointments appear, parties here and there, tomorrow's school project and next week's vacation. As we lay our lives out on paper (or screen!) it's easy to forget that we don't own these days. We don't will the sun to rise or the stars to appear. We know what we think a day will look like, but there's only One who sees it all, and His story is more magnificent than anything we could ever write. So let's hold our plans with open hands, prayerfully trusting Him with the details. Let's remember these squares are being strung together in love, one day at a time. Our little schedule is being swept up into a bigger, more beautiful picture than we could ever imagine.

You can make many plans, but the
Lord's purpose will prevail.
PROVERBS 19:21 NLT

MARCH 14

You're on your very own God-paved journey. Enjoy the steps today! Don't overthink them; simply live them with trust. Trust in His love for you, His constant care of you, His joy in seeing your joy. Peace is a provision that comes with putting God first—and putting Him first is the path to success.

In everything you do, put God first, and He will direct you and crown your efforts with success.
PROVERBS 3:6 TLB

MARCH 15

Latte or iced coffee? Turquoise or gray? So many daily decisions to make! Making choices is something you've labored over before, and not just for your coffee. Which school will be best-suited for your child? How can you choose the most adequate work transportation? Where should your family serve and minister? Decision-making requires wisdom and guidance from God. You know this deep within your heart, but it's so easy to forget in the moment. What if you stopped to ask Him for wisdom right now? Your delight in Him will result in fresh breaths of truth and light for decision making!

Behold, you delight in truth in the inward being,
and you teach me wisdom in the secret heart.
PSALM 51:6 ESV

MARCH 16

Start your day by looking at the good. Think of the good. Believe it's going to get even better. When God promises to fill your life with good things, get ready to be overtaken! His measure is more than you can ask or imagine. That's something to be happy about even though you can't fathom how amazing it will be.

He fills my life with good things!
PSALM 103:5 TLB

MARCH 17

Ever feel like you're living the same day over and over and over again? The dishes, the carpooling, the laundry never seem to stop. Motherhood can be a treadmill of never-changing scenery without much change in the results. The ancient Jews experienced this same feeling with worship. Their priests would sacrifice animals day after day, and still the horrifying action never erased the sins of the people. Jesus, the perfect Lamb of God, came to earth to stop this conveyer belt of sin. He lived a perfect life, died on the cross, and came back to life so we could be with Him forever. Next time you finally get to the bottom of a laundry basket or your dishwasher is actually empty, use it to remember that Jesus finished the work set for Him. He said, "It is finished," and forgave our sins with His last breath.

Every priest stands day after day ministering and offering the same sacrifices time after time, which can never take away sins. But this man, after offering one sacrifice for sins forever, sat down at the right hand of God.

HEBREWS 10:11–12 HCSB

MARCH 18

Dare to trust God with all your heart. Give Him the stuff you worry about, the clutter keeping you awake at night, the distractions throughout the day. Every burden you carry steals moments of peace that come from God carrying you. He puts our life moments in order for a reason—so we don't miss the present, right-in-front-of-us cries for a love that heals, a hope that holds, and a shelter that stays.

Trust in Him at all times. Pour out your heart to Him, for God is our refuge.
PSALM 62:8 NLT

MARCH 19

Whether we have one kid or ten kids, life will be as busy as we let it be. No matter who we are or what our situation, God gives all of us the same amount of time to steward each day. How are we using the time we've been given? A quick glance at our calendars is pretty revealing. As mothers, we'll find it loaded with all kinds of kid-related activities like school, practices, games, performances, summer camps, doctor appointments, play dates, birthday parties, and family fun nights. All good things, but whew! Between our own schedules and theirs, some days (or weeks or months, if we're to be completely honest) it's nearly impossible to catch our breath. When was the last time you scheduled downtime? When was the last time you slowed down long enough to put an appointment with God on your calendar? Let today be the day.

Be still, and know that I am God!

PSALM 46:10 NLT

MARCH 20

The thought of God keeping us in perfect peace if we think about Him often sounds like a pretty perfect exchange. Days are rarely without bumps, stresses, and challenges, so to know we're a thought—a moment—away from the quiet, calming presence of God is enough to face the day with courage. Trust is letting go of our cares to let God care for everything—and that is a powerful, peace-filled promise.

He will keep in perfect peace all those who trust in Him, whose thoughts turn often to the Lord!
ISAIAH 26:3 TLB

MARCH 21

Home school, private school, public school? How much screen time? How much sugar? Which activities are best for our kids? Which friendships? Oh, the decisions that come with raising a family! And because we each have a unique mix of backgrounds, circumstances, strengths, and struggles, our answers to life's questions are bound to be different. It's tempting to judge others for their choices or compare ourselves to them, wishing we could be different or better. The good news is, God didn't make cookie cutter people, and He doesn't expect us to fit into the same mold. (How boring would that be?!) As we prayerfully seek His will and listen for His guidance, we don't have to worry what our neighbor is doing. We're free to encourage one another on the journey and celebrate the countless ways He shows up in all our lives.

Live in harmony with one another.
ROMANS 12:16 ESV

MARCH 22

The truth about giving kindness and goodness is that it's really about "getting" it—that life is hard at times and sometimes we forget that it's not about us. We live it, but we can't give it, and being kind and good and loving are the best ways to point hearts to the One who can.

Trust in the Lord and do good.
PSALM 37:3 NLT

MARCH 23

Feelings of guilt and shame wash over you as you sit in line. The alarm snooze button seemed especially enticing this morning. You rushed out the door, forgetting to even breathe a prayer of thanks for another day. One awesome thing about God? He is everywhere. And one more thing? He always forgives. Could you take a moment to embrace His presence right where you are? This is abiding. While we aren't perfect, our fruit-bearing comes when we stick with Him through thick and thin. Snooze button and all.

Whoever abides in me and I in him, he it is that bears much fruit, for apart from me you can do nothing.
JOHN 15:5 ESV

MARCH 24

Whatever today holds, know God is holding you. From the first waking moment to the crawling or falling into bed, He's got you in His hands because He loves you with all His heart. It might not go perfectly; and patience might run out; and faith is going to be tested. But God is close with the grace you need—and He'll be strong when you can't.

I am the First and Last; there is no other God.
ISAIAH 44:6 TLB

MARCH 25

How did moms make it before the Internet? How would they find a recipe for the four random items in their pantry at the last minute? How would they figure out the best way to get a cranky child to sleep or get their kid on a chore chart that works? Being a mom, no matter how many kids you have or how old they are, is always daunting. Every mom always wishes for a little bit of instruction as she walks through life with her kids. The good news is God has instruction waiting for us. Even more than instruction, God promises to advise us with grace and wisdom. And one step further? For the mama who barely has time to take a breath or sip a cup of tea before bed? God promises to instruct our hearts and minds while we sleep. We don't need to long for more insightful blog posts; the God of all wisdom has promised to advise, teach, counsel, and instruct us when we need it—even if it's when our heads hit the pillow at night!

I will praise the LORD who counsels me—
even at night my conscience instructs me.
PSALM 16:7 HCSB

MARCH 26

When it's hard to get up and not give up, there's strength standing ready to give you what you need—and remind your heart why God needs you. There are lives in the world you're made to love by reflecting the love that made you. And with His love comes protection, powered by a perfect Savior. You can't be replaced—and you won't find a place more empowering than His love.

He fills me with strength and
protects me wherever I go.
PSALM 18:32 TLB

MARCH 27

There are some parts of parenting that are ridiculously repetitive and routine. So many things we do on a daily basis are necessary, but just plain b-o-r-i-n-g. Doing laundry, washing dishes, changing diapers, sweeping cereal off the floor (again), packing school lunches, making dinner, taking our kids to another practice. It's easy to get sucked into the monotony of it all and forget that what we do every day matters. It matters to our family, because we are meeting practical needs. It matters to God because He is the One who gave us the family to care for in the first place.

We have a great opportunity in our day-to-day duties to demonstrate what it looks like to be good stewards of the ordinary, and how to have a good and grateful attitude while doing things that aren't exciting and entertaining. Do your to-do list in the name of the Lord!

And whatever you do, in word or in deed, do everything in the name of the Lord Jesus, giving thanks to God the Father through Him.
COLOSSIANS 3:17 HCSB

MARCH 28

To be known is such a sweet way to be loved. God knows you, and, wow, does He love you—like no one on earth ever will and more than anything in the universe that can be measured. And it isn't just our grace-washed, love-rebuilt inside—God loves our dust-particle, time-sensitive outside too—our humanness that needs Him daily to forgive and fix and strengthen. Lean hard into His all-consuming love today, trusting it knows your every need.

You know me inside and out...You know exactly how I was made.
PSALM 139:15 THE MESSAGE

MARCH 29

What comes to our minds when we hear the words "living water?" Maybe we see a clear stream filled with all kinds of life, rippling down a mountain. Or the breathtaking view of an ocean with its powerful waves and ever-changing shoreline. What we probably don't picture is a mud puddle or a plastic kiddie pool filled with stagnant sludge. There's no life, no movement, no wonder in that. (Other than the toddler who jumps in for a splash!) When Jesus spoke of living water to the woman at the well, He must've had a twinkle in His eye. Because what He's offering is wondrous. It's the kind of life that others can't help but be drawn to—beautiful, dynamic, filled with never-ending discovery. What He's offering is Himself, and there's no end to the depths or heights of life in Him.

Anyone who believes in Me may come and drink! For the Scriptures declare, "Rivers of living water will flow from his heart."
JOHN 7:38 NLT

MARCH 30

Let our hands reach into the lives of others with God's love and nothing more. No expectations or judgments, no agendas or questions. Just a continuous stream of heaven's love seeping from our smile and our words and the things we do. There isn't anything more important today. Love is all and it's what we all need. It guides every heart to a glorious Savior and does nothing but good.

Work with enthusiasm, as though you were working for the Lord rather than for people.
EPHESIANS 6:7 NLT

MARCH 31

Would you rather have a friend who needs the last word or a friend whose goal is to help you feel heard? Would you rather talk with someone whose fuse is short or someone who doesn't even carry matches that would light the fuse?

One of the best ways to be a good friend is to be the kind of friend you yourself would like to have. It takes practice, which means you have to take risks. You have to get out there. Make some mistakes. Find yourself in a sticky situation or conflict, and don't shy away. Instead, determine to be the kind of friend who wants to see things through in love.

Everyone must be quick to hear, slow to speak and slow to anger.
JAMES 1:19 NASB

APRIL 1

"How could I be so stupid?"

You can be so hard on yourself for the little things. No one else knows your inner dialogue and you don't want them to know.

Negative self-talk can be such a battle. The thoughts form and before you know it, you've called yourself unhealthy and unholy names.

But Jesus calls you beautiful. Loved. Worthy of His pursuit.

You are His chosen daughter. Just as your heavenly Father extends grace to you, so do you have the power to give grace to yourself. He accepts you as you are and sees you as you are in Him. His grace is enough.

But by God's grace I am what I am, and His grace toward me was not ineffective.
I CORINTHIANS 15:10 HCSB

APRIL 2

He's incredibly full of love for us, our Savior. Spilled on the cross, His love became salvation for every seeking soul. And what the seeking souls need to see in us is Him, the Holy One who makes them whole—with love that's perfect and personal, unconditional and unending, full and forgiving. Let that be our longing today: emulating His example.

Be full of love for others, following the example of Christ.
EPHESIANS 5:2 TLB

APRIL 3

Before cell phones, your best friend would call you at home and if you weren't there, your little brother would take a message. You'd get home late so you couldn't call her back. The next day, you'd return her call a full twenty-four hours after she originally called you. Whew! Today, phone call return time is about twenty minutes, and even then people start getting impatient!

King David knew this same feeling when he called out to God in song. He felt like the Lord wasn't listening, that God wouldn't fix his problem or give him the answer. Ever felt that way with God? God does promise to listen and answer. He doesn't ignore your call, put you on hold, or send you to voicemail. He hears your whispered prayer, your loud demands and desperate calls. He will answer through His Holy Spirit, His Word, and even by orchestrating miracles for you!

Know that the LORD has set apart his faithful servant for Himself; the LORD hears when I call to Him.
PSALM 4:3 NIV

APRIL 4

Be fearless today. Absolutely nothing is going to stop God's plan for you or stall His purposes in you. You might think you have to accomplish more, that the routine of your days can't be part of the real plan. But God can make anything happen from anywhere, anytime that He chooses. And since you're chosen, believe you're right where you belong—and be the brightest reflection of Him you can be.

Fear not, for I am with you and will bless you.
GENESIS 26:24 TLB

APRIL 5

One of the most beautiful gifts of being a mother is knowing our children like no one else does. The process of raising them day-in and day-out allows us to notice things about them that others wouldn't. We know when something small is really a big deal. We know when something hurts, even though they pretend it doesn't. God gives us glimpses into the most intricate parts of their hearts, yet we know instinctively that the best parts of our children have nothing to do with us. They are who they are in spite of us. Take some time to marvel at your children today. Take note of their unique personalities. Take a breath and wonder at their abilities. Take a moment to explain to them how amazing you think they are. Take their face in your hands and tell them it's a blessing to be their mom.

You created my inmost being; You knit me together in my mother's womb.
PSALM 139:13 NIV

APRIL 6

If we start our day with the mind-set that everything we do matters, everything we do will make a difference. Life is made up of ordinary moments only God sees. These are extraordinary opportunities to worship, to listen, to be still, and to get our hearts saturated with love before pouring into the hundreds of daily things to come. The work of the Master is always about love. Let the things you do point the world to Him.

Throw yourselves into the work of the Master, confident that nothing you do for Him is a waste of time or effort.
I CORINTHIANS 15:58 THE MESSAGE

APRIL 7

Here's a fun way to remind kids (and kids at heart!) to fix our eyes on Jesus. Stand facing one another, bring one foot up as high as you can, and see who can balance the longest. There's one rule: Keep your eyes on another person. Notice how difficult it can be to steady yourself while gazing at a moving target.

Now try again while everyone looks at a fixed point on the wall, or in the distance. It's much easier to balance when our eyes are locked in on something immovable. That's Jesus. When we start feeling unsettled or unsure, out of balance or discouraged in life, it's often because we've lost sight of the One who steadies us. Let's remember in those moments to turn our hearts toward Him, our firm foundation in an ever-changing world.

Keeping our eyes on Jesus, the source and perfecter of our faith.
HEBREWS 12:2 HCSB

APRIL 8

Shine the love of God on your corner of the world, toward the faces that are in front of you daily, on that holy ground called home. The challenge to love is maybe a little more real here at times, in the comfort of raw emotions and our real selves. Be kind here first. Always. And trust God to strengthen the love inside the four walls so there will be plenty of courage to love outside them.

Let your light shine...! For the glory of the Lord is streaming from you.
ISAIAH 60:1 TLB

APRIL 9

"I can do it all by myself," she states firmly.

In this moment, you realize that your baby is growing up, and soon she'll do more than go potty on her own. While longing to foster independence and growth, you hover close by, ready to assist at any moment. The thought crosses your mind that parenting has taught you so much about your God. Her words that she can do it alone help you remember your total reliance on God. Yes, He is your help, hovering close. He's ready to assist you at any moment. He longs to be the One you turn to. He'll keep you going, especially as you mature in your faith.

God is my helper; the Lord is the sustainer of my life.
PSALM 54:4 HCSB

APRIL 10

It's going to be harder some days, this grace walk. We won't feel deserving and maybe we won't see a way through. But God sees you on the other side of the difficult days and the discouragement, because He's carrying you there—and when He puts your feet back on the ground, see how you've grown even stronger still.

We never give up…our inner strength
in the Lord is growing every day.
II CORINTHIANS 4:16 TLB

APRIL 11

Choosing the best disciplinary act for a disobedient child sometimes feels like drawing out of a hat. What would be best? Taking his lovey? Sending her to her room? Sitting in time-out? A spanking?! Discipline sometimes seems too hard to be worth it. The tears, the anger, the whininess are almost worse than the infraction that started it. God set up discipline to be good, and not just discipline from a smart mom to a disobedient child.

In the Psalms, we read that we are blessed when God disciplines us! We are blessed because it gives God the opportunity to teach us His law. When He does, we will have relief from our trouble. Just as we long for our children to understand the love and good we have behind discipline, God longs for us to see the same and feel relief from the pain of sin.

Lord, happy is the man You discipline and teach from Your law to give him relief from troubled times until a pit is dug for the wicked.
PSALM 94:12–13 HCSB

APRIL 12

We've all had them, days when the burdens bearing down make it hard to get up and start the day. The covers over our eyes feel right in moments that ache deeply, untouched by words. Our hearts find a faint prayer: *Where do we go from here?* We go to the One who knew we'd need a hiding place, so He became one. Away from the world and the worries, God holds us tight, all the way back to hope again, comforting until the storm calms. No matter how difficult the day, God is with us to make a way.

You are my hiding place from every storm of life.
PSALM 32:7 TLB

APRIL 13

Have you ever observed a team who has the right people in the right positions at the right time? It's amazing to see people working together to achieve a common goal. Maybe you've seen a teacher open the eyes of their students to a new concept; maybe you've watched a coach lead their team to a championship; maybe you've witnessed a pastor gathering their sheep to meet a need in the world; or maybe you've listened to a conductor unifying a symphony.

Working together is God's perfect plan for His people, and that includes families too. Are you in awe over the group of people God has placed in your own home? Do you appreciate their unique gifts and talents instead of letting their differences drive you crazy? God-given gifts are good on their own, but they are even better when working together. That's the beautiful body of Christ!

The human body has many parts, but
the many parts make up one whole body.
So it is with the body of Christ.
I CORINTHIANS 12:12 NLT

APRIL 14

Schedules demand, time flies, and quiet eludes. Invite God to bring the calm. Is calmness even possible? Only with His love—a love that, when we welcome it and surrender to it, makes it impossible for us to be fearful, frazzled, or fed up. When stress presses in, take a second to breathe deeply, say Jesus's name, and know love's calming effect. Doing so has a beautiful way of connecting us to our Lord so our actions reveal Him to others.

He'll calm you with His love.
ZEPHANIAH 3:17 THE MESSAGE

APRIL 15

Watching kids open Christmas sweaters can be comical. They're practical, they're warm...but really, Mom? Boring! We all have our idea of what a good gift might be at the holidays—and in life. But when the wrapping comes off and it's not what we were hoping for, how do we react? Maybe it's a new job or better school, a fun family opportunity or a big change that we just knew would make our lives a whole lot easier. It's natural to feel disappointed when our high hopes don't pan out. It's good to give ourselves time to process—but then it's vital to move on. If God allows a door to close, we can trust 100 percent that He has something better waiting, all in His time. It's up to us to find joy in what is, and trust Him expectantly to reveal what will be.

Every generous act and every perfect gift is from above.
JAMES 1:17 HCSB

APRIL 16

Happiness comes as we seek after God. Put differently, living happily happens when we long to be where we belong—in Him—doing exactly what He created us to do: love! Love is always just and good, and God's love is all that we need to change the world as His love changes us. The more we give, the more we grow—and the more we glow!

Happy are those who long to be just and good,
for they shall be completely satisfied.
MATTHEW 5:6 TLB

APRIL 17

Little ones love makeup. They love having their nails painted, and giggle gleefully when the tiniest bit of glittery eyeshadow is brushed across their lids.

As a mom, you know beauty is not only skin deep. You want your kids to feel beautiful not because of their long eyelashes and curly hair, but because of the One who placed beauty deep within their souls. We are all invited to add to the beauty of God's story. The invitation comes straight from the One who created beauty itself, and it's also extended to our kids. We can all be the beautiful feet that bear good news. As our hearts reflect the love and beauty of God, our faces (and feet) become beautiful without a hint of makeup or polish.

And how will anyone go and tell them without being sent? That is why the Scriptures say, "How beautiful are the feet of messengers who bring good news!"

ROMANS 10:15 NLT

APRIL 18

Today let's not be pulled along by the pressures of this world but instead be guided by God's grace and love! We're going to let love lead the way, helping us choose our words and know how to act. We're going to slow down on the emotional front and instead use our spiritual fortitude—for God's Spirit in us always draws from and delivers love.

Let love guide your life.
COLOSSIANS 3:14 TLB

APRIL 19

Tough news wrecks your heart, and fear threatens to overtake you. What does this mean for the future?

Whether health issues, moving, relationship problems, or other stresses, the future doesn't have to be feared. No matter the obstacles, God has a plan greater than the problem. He makes a way when there is no way. His purposes for you are greater than any predicament you encounter. His promises of fulfillment supersede any fear of the future! Take a moment to savor His love and devotion for you.

The Lord will fulfill His purpose for me. Lord, Your love is eternal; do not abandon the work of Your hands.

PSALM 138:8 HCSB

APRIL 20

What you go through in life, you will never go through alone. From the tears that fall in the quiet hours to the sadness you feel closing in at times, God sees it all—and He's moving things into place that you can't see now but will. You'll see your hopes come to life, you'll see your desires unfold, and you'll see God's love for you in a way you've never seen before.

God has said, "I will never, never fail you nor forsake you."
HEBREWS 13:5 TLB

APRIL 21

Be thankful for the work God is doing in you even when it's difficult. Choose joy on days that aren't easy. Hold on to your faith with both hands and know that your heart is growing stronger. Every moment of your life is sifted through God's love and what's going to open your eyes to more of it.

When troubles of any kind come your way, consider it an opportunity for great joy. For you know that when your faith is tested, your endurance has a chance to grow.
JAMES 1:2–3 NLT

APRIL 22

Parenting books can fill a bookshelf, stack up on a bedside table, and spout all kinds of wisdom for child-rearing. We can glean terrific ideas from each of them depending on our own style and personality. God has also given us a foolproof, simple way to lead our children. When Paul wrote his letter to the people living in Colossae, he encouraged them to let the "message of Christ dwell among you richly" and to teach each other with psalms, hymns, and songs from the Spirit. Now, isn't that a lovely way to teach your kids? With songs based on God's Word! Use the book of Psalms as your guide and speak your favorites to and over your children. Seek out God's Word written to music and play it over them. Let God's Word dwell in you richly and it will be rich in your children too!

Let the message of Christ dwell among you richly as you teach and admonish one another with all wisdom through psalms, hymns, and songs from the Spirit, singing to God with gratitude in your hearts.
COLOSSIANS 3:16 NIV

APRIL 23

Every path has purpose. Even the ones with pit-falls and pity parties we throw in solitude when our minds fill up with why and how much longer? If we want God's fullness, we have to trust Him fully. And what He sees that we can't is the moment our hearts are ready for the great things He has planned for us.

My purpose is to give life in all its fullness.
JOHN 10:10 TLB

APRIL 24

Being a mother involves repeating instructions… over and over again. We ask our children everything from "Please go brush your teeth" to "Please ask me before you invite a friend over to spend the night." And even though we think we have been as clear as we can be, they still need frequent reminders of our expectations. We rack our brain to find other ways to reinforce what we are trying to teach them. We say it in different ways on different days, and we even buy cute signs to hang on our walls to remind them. How often are we repeating and reinforcing the instruction of Scripture like that? As children of God, we all need daily reminders of His expectations. So if we're going to sound like a broken record, let the lyrics of the song we're playing come straight from the Word of God.

You must commit yourselves wholeheartedly to these commands that I am giving you today. Repeat them again and again to your children. Talk about them when you are at home and when you are on the road, when you are going to bed and when you are getting up.

DEUTERONOMY 6:6–7 NLT

APRIL 25

Peace will come, joy will surface, hope will emerge, and our hearts will rest when we give God control and focus on Him. Don't we want His infinite goodness? Yes, we do, but sometimes we go our own way and bury our wounded and wayward hearts in worldly things. But He stands at the ready for our undivided attention, responding to it with His immeasurable grace.

He surrounds me with loving-kindness and tender mercies. He fills my life with good things!
PSALM 103:4–5 TLB

APRIL 26

It's not fair! I was here first! Hey, their half is bigger! We may hear these words from kids now and then, but if we're honest with ourselves, grown-ups have ways of whining too. In traffic, at work, dealing with relationships, finances—you name it! We so often forget about the lavish grace we ourselves have received. But here's an idea: What if we become intentional about giving grace, even in the most frustrating situations? That pushy guy in traffic? Let him in. The person who bought the thing we couldn't afford? Give them a sincere compliment. The rude customer service lady? Be gentle with her. Everyone has a story. Few things reveal God's heart to the world today like giving radical grace. There are plenty of opportunities, and who knows? It just may become our new favorite thing to do!

Freely you have received; freely give.
MATTHEW 10:8 NKJV

APRIL 27

Trust that God is right here, right now. You are never alone. You are never ignored. God is paying close attention to everything that concerns you...the sad, the happy, and every moment in between. Today there will be glimpses of His love sent just for you. Look for every one of them and let them make your heart feel loved.

Trust your lives to the God who created you, for He will never fail you.
I PETER 4:19 NLT

APRIL 28

Using words to bring out the best in others takes letting God bring out the best in us. How does He speak to us? "You are precious to me and honored, and I love you" (Isaiah 43:4 TLB). It doesn't get any more gracious than that. If we put a "grace guard" on our conversations, there would be a lot more smiles in the world...and a lot of hearts feeling loved.

Be gracious in your speech. The goal is to bring out the best in others in a conversation, not put them down, not cut them out.
COLOSSIANS 4:6 THE MESSAGE

APRIL 29

It's easy to both burn the midnight oil and wake up with the sun when you've got little kids underfoot. There's always something more to get done! Moms don't get a lot of rest. Often we even forget that God promises rest. Real rest. The kind that allows us to catch our breath, to laugh, to feel peaceful. It may be hard to find pockets of peace during our crazy days, but you can creatively make space to feel His peace. Create moments for rest in the midst of your day, squishing them in and around your regular happenings. Pray in the preschool pickup line. Write the Word during your lunch break. Make it work for you. You can do this, and you will be all the better for resting in His presence.

The LORD replied, "My Presence will go with you, and I will give you rest."
EXODUS 33:14 NIV

APRIL 30

The moments when we're mindful of God will always make a difference. When it doesn't seem like the ordinary course of our day is ordered by God, we have to believe with all our hearts that it is. When we start to feel that the path God paves must be more elaborate, we need to recall the steps of our Savior—personal interactions, sharing meals, telling stories. Simple things can often make the most significant, and eternal, impressions.

The Lord your God will bless you…
in all the work of your hands.
DEUTERONOMY 16:15 NKJV

MAY 1

His head hangs low and you can tell by his walk that something is wrong. "Mom, Matthew said Susie was a bad reader. I told him that wasn't very nice to say, so he wouldn't play with me at recess."

Flashback to third grade when you encountered a similar situation. "Choosing friends can be tricky. The best way I know to have friends is to be a good friend. Have you noticed anyone in the class who likes to say good things about others? I would choose to play with her on the playground tomorrow."

Father, thank You for guidance. Help both of us to be good friends to others and show Your love.

The one who walks with the wise will become wise.
PROVERBS 13:20 HCSB

MAY 2

You have a new day in front of you, full of possibility—with God, maybe an impossibility too. Miracles happen in moments. Press on and keep believing if you're believing for something only He can make happen. When it gets here, your faith will start a wildfire in you that spreads like crazy because the world is going to see the truth burning: God keeps His promises—and promises His best.

With God nothing will be impossible.
LUKE 1:37 NKJV

MAY 3

"When am I going to be the Good Mom? Will my kids turn out right? What do I need to do to actually get this mom thing right once in a while?" We've all asked the questions—sometimes on a daily basis! The overwhelming responsibility of motherhood can wear us down, making us feel defeated. When Joshua becomes the new leader of Israel (the parent, so to speak), God only gives him a few instructions. The first is to be strong and courageous! (Good idea for moms, too!) The second is to speak God's Word and think about it all the time. It's a simple task but with an immense reward as God promises Joshua prosperity and success! Let's do the same with God's Word—keeping it on our lips, meditating on it day and night, being careful to do everything written in it so we can be prosperous and successful in motherhood!

Keep this Book of the Law always on your lips; meditate on it day and night, so that you may be careful to do everything written in it. Then you will be prosperous and successful.

JOSHUA 1:8 NIV

MAY 4

Do you need a hand today? The God who counts the stars and counts every life priceless is holding your hand, so fear has to go. You have all the help you'll need to walk smoothly through the rough patches and stand tall in the face of things that bring your heart down. You can live the moments happily, hopefully, and full to the top with love. Have that kind of day—you have God holding you.

I am holding you by your right hand....
Don't be afraid; I am here to help you.
ISAIAH 41:13 TLB

MAY 5

A masterpiece is considered priceless for multiple reasons, but mainly because of the person who created it. The artist is considered a master of their craft. They are highly respected in their field and revered by their peers. People gaze upon their work with wonder and awe. They study their techniques and mimic their style. Have you ever thought about God as an artist? His body of work is made up of every person that ever was and that ever will be. The world is His living gallery, and He has filled it with priceless pieces of art. That includes you! You were born in His holy imagination long before He created the canvas of your life. Do you see yourself from the eyes of your Creator? Reminder: He declared you a masterpiece worth dying for. Live from that truth!

We are God's masterpiece. He has created us anew in Christ Jesus, so we can do the good things He planned for us long ago.
EPHESIANS 2:10 NLT

MAY 6

You are loved, appreciated, brave, and one-of-a-kind. This is a God-designed day, written for you. It might call on the courage He's grown in you through challenges or the strength that's come through brokenness and a thousand tears. He holds you up for others to see because you held Him while the battle raged. Be a light today—you're shining brighter than ever before.

Be strong! Be courageous!... For the Lord your God will be with you.
DEUTERONOMY 31:6 TLB

MAY 7

Asking for help. Why is it so hard for us sometimes? It may be one of these: (1) We see our need for others as weakness. But we know God says differently. From creating Adam's helper (Genesis 2:18) to calling the body of Christ to be "members of one another" (Romans 12:5), partnership has always been part of His design. (2)We don't want to let go of control. Asking for help means taking the risk that someone will want to do it their way. If they're willing to bless us with support, let's be willing to receive with grace. (3) We never learned it was okay. This is an important one to remember as moms: If we're always trying to go it alone, our kids get the message that being grown up means not needing anyone. Let's show them otherwise. Helping them learn to do life with others is one of the greatest gifts we can give.

Carry one another's burdens; in this way you will fulfill the law of Christ.
GALATIANS 6:2 HCSB

MAY 8

Every day is a fresh start and a new opportunity to let the past go and let God lead. All day long and especially on the long days, there's nothing more healing than hoping in Him. He leads with love that doesn't stop when we slip, strength that doesn't slip when we struggle, and the Holy Spirit, who never struggles to stay right with us through it all.

Lead me by Your truth and teach me,
for You are the God who saves me. All
day long I put my hope in You.
PSALM 25:5 NLT

MAY 9

Kids love playing dress-up. On any given day there may be princesses, superheroes, and knights running around the living room. As they dress up and play pretend, we have a chance to remind them that God made them warriors. That's right! God has given us an unbreakable and hefty armor. In chapter 6 of Ephesians, God tells us to suit up. He provides us a shield of faith to fend off evil and protect against painful blows. He gives us a belt of truth, a breastplate of righteousness, and a helmet of salvation—all of which help us reject the pointed lies of evil. Finally, God offers us the sword of the Spirit, which is His powerful Word. Once we're suited up in our armor? We are free to live with God, for God, because of God's love. Warriors indeed!

Therefore put on the full armor of God, so that when the day of evil comes, you may be able to stand your ground, and after you have done everything, to stand. Stand firm then, with the belt of truth buckled around your waist, with the breastplate of righteousness in place, and with your feet fitted with the readiness that comes from the gospel of peace. In addition to all this, take up the shield of faith, with which you can extinguish all the flaming arrows of the evil one. Take the helmet of salvation and the sword of the Spirit, which is the word of God.

EPHESIANS 6:13–17 NIV

MAY 10

Jesus paid for our freedom and the wonderful things God freely gives. Grace is overwhelming for a reason—it's much too good to keep to ourselves. Give some away today. Give a little love to every person you see. Give kindness every chance you get. Give your time to someone in need, even though it interrupts your plans. Our plans will never be more important than the chances God gives us to share His love.

We have received God's Spirit…so we can know the wonderful things God has freely given us.
I CORINTHIANS 2:12 NLT

MAY 11

You didn't mean to allow them, but the angry words poured from your mouth before you could filter them. It seemed too late; the damage was done. What now? While it's tempting to belittle yourself and wish for a do-over, now is the time to see yourself as God sees you. He never belittles or berates, but longs to see a humble heart. "Lord, I'm sorry. Please forgive me. Provide healing words to soothe the wound and usher in Your peace." Take a minute to rest in God's faithful forgiveness.

If we confess our sins, he is faithful and just to forgive us our sins and to cleanse us from all unrighteousness.
I JOHN 1:9 ESV

MAY 12

Now is what matters. Always. We can't see ahead, and we can't change what's behind, but God can. Not only is He pulling our hearts in the direction of His best, He's taking the past, when we fell out of step with His will, and turning it into something good—a stronger soul, a deeper understanding of grace. With God, all is good now, or it will be. We just live the moments and trust.

God sees into my heart right now.
I CORINTHIANS 13:12 TLB

MAY 13

It's the same every day: you've made breakfast and packed lunches before you've had your morning coffee. You've tied shoes, ironed uniforms, and found jackets before you've slipped off your slippers. You've watched cartoons, told stories, and played with toys before you've even checked your social media. When will you get some rest and quiet of your own? When will someone take care of you?

God made women in His image, so He uses feminine descriptions of Himself to show us how He cares for us. In Psalm 91, the writer compares God to a bird covering us with His feathers, where His wings are a refuge to us. Think of a brood of chicks under a hen's wings—safe, secure, and unencumbered. This is what God does and wants to do for you. Take a break with Him, slide under His feathers, cozy up under His wings to find the refuge you need.

He will cover you with His feathers; you will take refuge under His wings.
PSALM 91:4 HCSB

MAY 14

Before a child grows up and learns to be more self-aware, smiles and laughs are a regular part of his day. Adults have a funny habit of making the strangest faces, doing everything they can to coax that baby grin to the surface. In their innocence, babies understand joy! That shouldn't change as we get older. Knowing God, understanding Him better, and receiving His love should lead to deeper and deeper joy. The kind that can't be shaken under any circumstances. God loves fun! Read Nehemiah 8:10 and Zephaniah 3:17 today. And find strength in His joy.

So I commended pleasure, for there is nothing good for a man under the sun except to eat and to drink and to be merry, and this will stand by him in his toils throughout the days of his life which God has given him under the sun.

ECCLESIASTES 8:15 NASB

MAY 15

Have you ever looked at your children and wondered with all sincerity how in the world those very different people came from the same two people? It's truly an outright miracle that every child that God places on this earth is a unique reflection of their parents. They inherit things from us like their looks, personalities, temperaments, and abilities. They also learn things from us, like habits and behavior. They are created in our image, yet no two are alike. The same is true with us as children of God. Just as children are a reflection of their parents, we too are a reflection of our heavenly Father. He created us in His image—so everything good we see in ourselves or others is God-given. Make it a practice to notice good and Godly things in your children and others, pointing out how they are a beautiful reflection of God!

So God created mankind in His own image,
in the image of God He created them;
male and female He created them.
GENESIS 1:27 NIV

MAY 16

Knowing you are trusted can be one of the best feelings in the world. From little girls telling secrets on the playground, to the highest government officials—we understand the power of confidence and trust.

So, how does it feel to know that you have the ear and the trust of your heavenly Father? That the God of the universe reveals His mysteries to you as you build your relationship with Him? In this way, life truly is like a treasure hunt of discovery. Like children wandering through the grass looking for the plastic eggs that Grandma has hidden, we get to enjoy and explore all the treasures of heaven when we know God.

The secret of the Lord *is for those who fear Him, and He will make them know His covenant.*
PSALM 25:14 NASB

MAY 17

It's tempting to skim through instruction manuals to save time. There's so much info—and who needs to know all that stuff anyway? But sometimes in our haste, we miss an important step that's necessary for everything else to run smoothly. God's Word about anger in James 1:19 is a perfect example. It all begins with listening. Genuine listening requires humility; it means letting go of our own agenda and pausing to truly hear the heart of the other person. Instead of formulating an answer while they're speaking, or cooking up a clever comeback, we give them space and grace to share what they need to (even if it's uncomfortable, frustrating, or downright mean).

Listening gives us a moment to rest in the presence of Jesus and let the Spirit take the lead. When that happens, it's much easier to hold our tongue and allow our potential anger to be transformed into compassion and loving action.

Everyone must be quick to hear, slow to speak, and slow to anger.
JAMES 1:19 HCSB

MAY 18

The heart that loves God becomes more like God—and He loves to give. It's not a matter of whether or not we have something to give: God is all-sufficient and, by the power of His Spirit living within His children, He is our Source for whatever He calls us to share. So when the door opens to reflect His love, or when He opens our eyes to a need we can meet because He has blessed us, may we happily serve one another because we faithfully serve Him.

The godly love to give!
PROVERBS 21:26 NLT

MAY 19

The staircase is dark and looming to a two-year-old. Her little feet push upward, but her pudgy hand can't reach the light switch. With the kind of determined, stubborn bravery found only in toddlers, she chooses to climb the staircase in the dark, deciding that reaching her goal is worth the moments of fear. Her final target, waiting at the top of the stairs in the light? Mommy.

Trusting God with all of your heart and thinking of Him in all your ways means opening your heart to His path, scary and new and untraveled as it may be. It means stepping forward in faith, taking one stair at a time until you're safe at the top, the darkness behind you. When you're not sure how to trust, know that God is waiting at the top with outstretched arms.

Trust in the Lord with all your heart, and do not rely on your own understanding;think about Him in all your ways, and He will guide you on the right paths.
PROVERBS 3:5–6 HCSB

MAY 20

There are times in the Bible where it says the Lord remembered someone in their distress, or God remembered them and acted. It's not that God forgets. But remembering can be like acknowledging a person at a certain point in time. God knows your every need and your every move. We, on the other hand, don't always remember God! But we have a promise. If we cry out to Him and seek Him, He will be there. He will help. Sometimes, though, we need to take the first step to get out of our emotions and self-centeredness. Remember God, and He will remember you.

The righteous cry, and the LORD hears and delivers them out of all their troubles.
PSALM 34:17 NASB

MAY 21

Fatigue is catching up with you, and the benefits of serving your family appear invisible. Lately the demands have grown in intensity and you're flat-out tired. While a few moments of rest are valuable, don't give up on loving and encouraging your children. You've got this, Mama. God is on your side and will give you the strength to continue the journey. It's okay to be tired, but remember your true strength comes from the Lord. He has a never-ending supply and your reward is on the horizon.

Let us not become weary in doing good,
for at the proper time we will reap a
harvest if we do not give up.
GALATIANS 6:9 NIV

MAY 22

There are many benefits of being a child of God. We're probably not truly aware of more than 5 percent of His presence in our lives! What if that detour on the road actually detoured you away from a bad accident? What if missing your flight meant striking up a valuable conversation with a fellow delayed traveler? What if going to that other grocery store on a whim put you in line to bless a sweet older woman by carrying her groceries out? God works in many amazing, sometimes obvious, and usually subtle ways. The more we open our eyes, the more He opens our eyes. And we begin to see the true beauty of the world around us.

When you pass through the waters, I will be with you; and through the rivers, they will not overflow you. When you walk through the fire, you will not be scorched, nor will the flame burn you.... Do not fear, for I am with you; I will bring your offspring from the east, and gather you from the west.

ISAIAH 43:2, 5 NASB

MAY 23

Are you concerned, maybe even worried about an aspect of your child's personality or behavior? Are you scared there might be sin already crouching at the door to their heart? Do you wonder if maybe you've missed something big that might grow into something even bigger? Maybe it's their overwhelming fear about every little thing, or their inability to be kind to a sibling or how they lie and manipulate at such a young age. There's no way to know what's in the heart and mind of your child. They are their own beautiful person, crafted by God. The best solution is to ask God to show you what is inside your child's heart. Go to Him in prayer, asking for wisdom, revelation, and clear understanding of the problem. God will respond generously! Even if it takes time and small steps, you can be sure God will give understanding to you.

If any of you lacks wisdom, you should ask God, who gives generously to all without finding fault, and it will be given to you.
JAMES 1:5 NIV

MAY 24

She had been a straight A student in high school, but college seemed to be falling to bits. She comes home smelling like smoke, refusing to participate in family activities. That smile you used to adore hasn't been seen on her face for a long time. *What happened to my baby?* you wonder.

God's love is the best. Better even than a parent's love for their children. His heart breaks when we turn away, and He rejoices when we accept His love with open arms.

We have the choice to remain in God's love. His heart is always wide open. He patiently waits if we turn away from Him. But it always feels best to accept His love and stay there.

Just as the Father has loved Me, I have also loved you; abide in My love.
JOHN 15:9 NASB

MAY 25

After spending forty days in the desert in His fully human state, Jesus was beyond hangry. He was without strength and literally starving. Yet every time He was tempted, He simply spoke the Word of God right out loud, directly in the face of His foe. His ability to resist temptation in such a weak state could only be the result of divine power. We have access to that same power! When we do the hard work and heart work of Scripture memory, the Holy Spirit can bring verses to mind in the heat of the moment or when hard decisions have to be made.

Does your family have a go-to verse to fight off temptation and prevent sin? If not, choose one to memorize today. It's worth the effort to be able to say, "Not today, Satan."

I have hidden Your word in my heart,
that I might not sin against You.
PSALM 119:11 NLT

MAY 26

How can laundry, cleaning up kid messes, and trying not to yell at the twins be my calling? she wonders hopelessly. Life sometimes feels like a mess, not a ministry. But the Lord loves her work. He grins when she gets down on the ground and plays with her sons and their action figures. His heart fills every time she folds her husband's shirts and puts them away. Because ultimately, He knows her heart. And she doesn't do life perfectly, but she does her best to love the Lord well through it all.

Whatever you do in word or deed, do all in the name of the Lord Jesus, giving thanks through Him to God the Father.
COLOSSIANS 3:17 NASB

MAY 27

Most of us have done it—tiptoed into a little one's room at night after all is quiet. They've run, climbed, played, laughed, cried, made messes and memories…and finally have surrendered to sleep. Soft breathing. Still hands. Sweet faces. We're filled with gratitude for their very being. We love them just because they are. Can we remember that we are children too? That our heavenly Father surrounds us, right in this moment, with a love beyond what we could ever imagine? No striving or struggle can earn it; no circumstance or choice can change it. In this busy, gotta-do-better, try-harder, live-faster world, it's hard to believe sometimes. You. Me. Just as we are. Like little girls resting in our daddy's loving gaze. Let's take a deep breath today and take it all in. (Repeat as necessary.)

Give thanks to the Lord, for He is good;
His faithful love endures forever.
I CHRONICLES 16:34 HCSB

MAY 28

Sometimes things happen just so God can show us who He really is. Sometimes we end up in situations that are tailor-made for our cries out to Him for help and understanding. Then when He delivers, it's so obvious where the help came from! How often do we forget to call on God in times of need? How often do we try to do things under our own steam, only to give up defeated and exhausted? The next time you find yourself striving, try dropping everything and crying out to Him. He may just have the answer you've been waiting for.

Now, O Lord our God, I pray, deliver us from his hand that all the kingdoms of the earth may know that You alone, O Lord, are God.
II KINGS 19:19 NASB

MAY 29

Sometimes it's all too much. The messes, the crumbs, the tantrums, and the never-ending laundry. The dishes, the potty training, and difficult bedtimes can sometimes feel like being a mom is just too much. Like God may have given us more than we can handle. But really, God doesn't give us more than He can handle.

Swap out "we" for "He" and there is truth. One letter changes everything.

We can't do anything on our own. But when clinging to Him...then we can carry on. It's by God's grace and with His patience that we can handle really hard days. He is always with you, and He is always in control when all seems chaotic.

And remember, I am with you
always, to the end of the age.
MATTHEW 28:20 HCSB

MAY 30

Do you know how strong you are? Do you truly realize what you're capable of? Most people probably don't know until they find themselves stretched to the limit. A mother experiences this as she gives birth. At the point of no return, the lion within roars up and surprises the victor!

"'Not by might, nor by power, but by My Spirit,' says the LORD" (Zechariah 4:6 NASB). Those who believe in Jesus have the same power that raised Him from the dead living in them. That's why when Jesus says that nothing will be impossible for those who believe, we can trust He knows what He's talking about.

From the days of John the Baptist until now
the kingdom of heaven suffers violence,
and violent men take it by force.
MATTHEW 11:12 NASB

MAY 31

She left her clothes on the floor again. He forgot his gym shoes. The bathroom looks like a bomb went off, and as you walk through the house, all you can think is, *A little help here?*

While family life can make mommas feel like superpowers are required, remembering where your help comes from is sometimes all you need. God is your help! Breathe this prayer to remember that He is the difference:

"Lord, thank You for being my help. Thank You for sustaining me through the mess, and help us get things in order."

Surely God is my help; the Lord is the one who sustains me.
PSALM 54:4 NIV

JUNE 1

Do you remember the story of King Jehoshaphat? He was king of Judah several generations after David. One day, he received a report of an enemy coming to attack. He called for a fast and gathered all the people—men, women, and children—at the temple to ask God to deliver them. God then told them not to be afraid but go into battle and see how He would defeat their enemy.

Very early the next morning, Jehoshaphat gathered his army. But before they went out, he also appointed men to go ahead of them singing praise and thanks to God for His holiness and love.

When they came to the place they were to fight, the enemy army was already dead on the ground. Do you have an enemy army staring you down? Don't fight them. Turn to God and worship Him first and only. Let Him do battle for you!

Do not be afraid or discouraged because of this vast number, for the battle is not yours, but God's.
II CHRONICLES 20:15 HCSB

JUNE 2

Genuine love speaks by doing. It goes out of its way to make someone else's way a little easier. Genuine love is empowered by God alone. If we want to love others without judgment or conditions, we will do so only by trusting God: He is the only One who can teach us to see our fellow human beings with His eyes. Only God can prompt in our hearts genuine affection for others.

Love each other with genuine affection, and take delight in honoring each other.
ROMANS 12:10 NLT

JUNE 3

Blessed assurance, Jesus is mine. O what a foretaste of glory divine. Heir of salvation, purchase of God. Born of His Spirit, washed in His blood. Perfect submission, all is at rest. I in my Savior am happy and blessed. Watching and waiting, looking above. Filled with His goodness, lost in His love. This is my story, this is my song. Praising my Savior all the day long.

The lyrics of this old hymn are personal to the hymn writer but are deeply relatable in the heart of every believer. It's our story and our song too! Read the words of the hymn again, slowly. Meditate on their meaning and take the time to feel the emotion of each phrase. Then sing it aloud to the Lord with gratitude for the gift of salvation through Jesus!

Let the message about the Messiah dwell richly among you, teaching and admonishing one another in all wisdom, and singing Psalms, hymns, and spiritual songs, with gratitude in your hearts to God.
COLOSSIANS 3:16 HCSB

JUNE 4

Picture a child you love, sitting at the table, working carefully on a piece of artwork. You glance at them each time you walk by, delighted to watch that little drawing come to life. But soon there's the crunching of paper, a frustrated sigh, footsteps stomping away. "What happened?" you ask as you pick up the paper, smoothing it out.

"It's terrible. I'm a bad artist. I'll never get it right," comes the answer.

Your heart aches at those words. You don't see a mess on that paper. You see creativity, uniqueness, potential. You see that little artist and all their efforts through loving, compassionate eyes. Our Father is the same. He sees the beauty in our chaos. When we see failure, He sees possibility. He gathers the scribbles of our lives, blesses them with love and grace, and turns them into masterpieces.

He has made everything beautiful in its time.
ECCLESIASTES 3:11 NIV

JUNE 5

Chasing perfection is a huge temptation. Hard as we try, we will never actually reach perfection, because the only perfect gifts come from God above. He is the only perfect One. While perfection seems appealing, real life beckons with warmth. Our kids won't remember being late to school or church, if the cookies burned, or if the bathroom floors were always clean. They will remember spending time with their mom, they will remember their cares and concerns being heard, and most of all, they'll remember how you made them feel. Start today. Drop the pursuit of perfection and chase holy instead.

Every good and perfect gift is from above, coming down from the Father of the heavenly lights, who does not change like shifting shadows.

JAMES 1:17 NIV

JUNE 6

Sometimes we expect God to show up in a certain way for us, but He's not there. Other times, He shows up in ways that we least expect. God doesn't fit in a box (or a tomb, for that matter). Nothing can hold Him back from unfolding His perfect plan. We don't often have angels showing up and clearing up our confusion. So the best thing we can do is train ourselves to discover Him where He chooses to be seen. The Lord speaks uniquely to each of us. As you learn who He is to you, how He communicates will become clearer. And you'll learn to love the way He invades your circumstances—whether you expect Him to or not.

The angel said to the women, "Do not be afraid; for I know that you are looking for Jesus who has been crucified. He is not here, for He has risen, just as He said. Come, see the place where He was lying."

MATTHEW 28:5-6 NASB

JUNE 7

You remember the moment you laid your eyes on him and immediately love washed over you. He's your baby, and now? He's headed to a new school! How could it be that all the years have led to this moment of independence on a newfound level? As quickly as the memories flood over your heart, fear rains down as well. *What if he feels sick? What if he forgets his homework?* Just as fear enters your mind, the Spirit ushers in the promise of God. There is no need to fear; God is in control and loves him more than you do. Rest in Him.

For God gave us a spirit not of fear but of power and love and self-control.
II TIMOTHY 1:7 ESV

JUNE 8

You've seen them—the moms stuffing their screaming children into car seats in the parking lot, and those brave ladies carrying their kids under one arm while the child flails in disobedience.

Maybe it was you trying to control the uncontrollable child. Didn't you just wish someone would swoop in and buckle that kid in for you? Jesus calls Himself the Good Shepherd in the book of John. In Isaiah, the Good Shepherd gathers those little lambs (I'm assuming the wild, uncontrollable ones) in His arms and carries them close to His heart. Then you know what He does? He doesn't shame the mama. Or roll His eyes at her inadequacy. He gently leads that mama along beside Him. He takes the lead and covers that mama with love. Next time you're feeling out of control (or your kid is!), look to your Good Shepherd. He'll tend to you, His precious lamb.

He tends His flock like a shepherd: He gathers the lambs in His arms and carries them close to His heart; He gently leads those that have young.
ISAIAH 40:11 NIV

JUNE 9

God never, ever goes back on His word. If you can find a promise written, if you remember a word given, then continue to thank God for those things and believe they will happen. His timetable may not line up perfectly with yours, but His intentions will not waver. "For as many as are the promises of God, in [Jesus] they are yes" (II Corinthians 1:20 NASB). The empty tomb was a sealing of the new covenant of hope and salvation. So take heart, friend. If you believe, you will receive every ounce of promise you've been given by a very great God.

Calling a bird of prey from the east, the man of My purpose from a far country. Truly I have spoken; truly I will bring it to pass. I have planned it, surely I will do it.

ISAIAH 46:11 NASB

JUNE 10

Are you in the habit of calling out all the good God has for your children? Are you regularly claiming His promises for them? The Bible is full of spectacular, true stories of fulfilled promises and Fatherly favor. Pray this everlasting blessing from Numbers over your own children today—the same one the Lord gave to Moses to speak over the children of Israel. Soak up the verbs used in this verse and notice how personal each one makes this Old Testament blessing. Think deeply about what you are asking God to do for your children, and then thank Him for what He's already done!

May the LORD bless you and protect you. May the LORD smile on you and be gracious to you. May the LORD show you His favor and give you His peace.
NUMBERS 6:24–26 NLT

JUNE 11

Kids love life-size mazes. Turn a bunch of them loose in one of those, and they're off on an epic adventure. There's usually a platform above where you can see the whole path laid out from beginning to end. So even if it takes a while or somebody gets scared, you don't worry for a moment. They can hear your voice: "Go right! Now, left!" And if all else fails, you know you're going in for the rescue. That's our life as God's children—paths laid out with twists and turns, unexpected detours and delightful surprises. We may freak out a little from time to time, but not the Father. No part of our journey is unknown to Him. One of God's names revealed in Genesis is El Roi, "the God who sees." Let's give thanks that we're seen, known, and loved by Him today.

She gave this name to the Lord who spoke to her: "You are the God who sees me."
GENESIS 16:13 NIV

JUNE 12

Many times in Scripture we're told not to worry. Just don't! But, you say, that must not apply in my situation. My son is being bullied and the teacher won't do anything. Or, if my husband doesn't find work soon, we'll lose our house. Worrying must count for something…right?! But when God says don't, He means it. That may feel defeating, but it should empower you! He never asks us to do what we can't, with His help. The next time you are prone to worry, be very deliberate about choosing thanks. Think of crazy things to be thankful for. Your dining room table! Boxed hair color! Your son's tender, compassionate heart! Thanks is sometimes the very best warfare.

Do not worry then, saying, "What will we eat?" or "What will we drink?" or "What will we wear for clothing?" For the Gentiles eagerly seek all these things; for your heavenly Father knows that you need all these things.
MATTHEW 6:31–32 NASB

JUNE 13

"Treasure every moment." How many times have moms heard this from well-meaning strangers? And how many times have moms gritted their teeth, smiling at that well-meaning stranger while thinking, *I'm not treasuring this particular moment right now!* Here is permission to not treasure the moment when you walk into a diaper-less, post-nap disaster, when you are physically longing for ten minutes of alone time, or when you just want to sleep through the night. Those are hard moments that don't need to be treasured but that can connect us to God in prayer and in leaning on His strength. Treasure your kids, and treasure certain moments while letting go of others. Store the sweet ones in your heart and release the difficult ones to Him.

Wherever your treasure is, there the desires of your heart will also be.
LUKE 12:34 NLT

JUNE 14

You've always wanted to be the grace-giver, but somehow, this time it's harder. The words said to you and actions performed against you feel overwhelming and hurtful. How can you keep from harboring anger and resentment, much less give the benefit of the doubt? Then you remember the grace God has given to you. He is so generous in His mercy toward you.

"Lord, help me keep my testimony and extend love and mercy through the hurt. Would You give me Your grace to reach beyond my capabilities? Amen."

A good name is to be chosen rather than great riches, and favor is better than silver or gold.
PROVERBS 22:1 ESV

JUNE 15

One daughter takes what she wants. She scrabbles around for goodies and sweets, grabs the toys she wants to play with, and assumes that when she wants to go to the park instead of to school it will happen. Another daughter waits to receive. She appreciates a full plate and a balanced day. On occasion, she asks kindly if a treat might be had after dinner, or a picnic might be a nice way to spend a Saturday. God's heart is for the gentle, meek, and mild. He waits for us, with grateful hearts, to open our hand and ask for what we desire. The closer you are to Him, the gentler you become. And the more He longs to be generous to you.

You do not have because you do not ask.
JAMES 4:2 NASB

JUNE 16

There are times when you can't deny the power and presence of God. There are other days when you can't be sure that God is anywhere in the vicinity. Motherhood can seem like the most misunderstood and most undesirable job. Who would want to claim the spit-up, the tantrums, the how-many-times-do-we-have-to-go-through this? Jesus would. In fact, Jesus does. Jesus sees all that we do as His. Not because He is a selfish dictator. Instead, it's because He's a loving, personal God. He is before all things. All things—ALL THINGS are held together in Him.

So, even the hardest nights, even the best days, all your highs and lows, Jesus sees them and knows them because He's holding them together. He holds you together. He will continue to hold you as you follow Him and lead your family.

And he is before all things, and in him all things hold together.
COLOSSIANS 1:17 ESV

JUNE 17

Whether we are watching TV, listening to music, reading a book, or talking to a friend, the words of others continually impact us. We are constantly letting language in our minds, and we are constantly letting language leave our mouths. How can we be a Godly example through the words we say in our homes? Do a language check. Have your words been encouraging today? What have you said that is good and helpful? What have you said that isn't? Do you need to ask for forgiveness from someone for harsh words? If so, consider letting your children be a witness to your apology, as some of our best teaching moments as mothers come out of how we respond when we fall short. They are listening to the things we say when we are right and when we are wrong, so let's be purposeful with our words…always.

Don't use foul or abusive language. Let everything you say be good and helpful, so that your words will be an encouragement to those who hear them.

EPHESIANS 4:29 NLT

JUNE 18

Have you ever had one of those days when a chain of things goes wrong for no apparent reason? Sometimes things just happen that way. Other times, you may sense that you're under attack. And that is very possible. The spiritual forces of this world are hard at battle. One would undermine God's plan. The other would protect it. The next time you feel like you're under attack, pray. Tell God your suspicions, and then say what the truth is. You are a child of God, who can't be harmed by the enemy. You can take back your territory and stand victorious every time.

For our struggle is not against flesh and blood, but against the rulers, against the powers, against the world forces of this darkness, against the spiritual forces of wickedness in the heavenly places.

EPHESIANS 6:12 NASB

JUNE 19

For many of us, social media can be a blessing and a burden. Sometimes it's a much-needed connection; other times, we wonder why we even get on. Maybe we struggle with comparing ourselves, feeling less-than; maybe we're tempted to judge those whose shoes we haven't walked in, or we find ourselves investing more time in virtual life than in the life God has given us right here, right now. Regardless, what if we try a simple step to help steer our hearts in the right direction each time we pick up a device? What if we take one deep breath, asking for the Holy Spirit to guide us and fill us in that moment? Let's redeem our screens—use them to encourage, lift up, and be filled up—with the true, noble, right, pure, lovely admirable, excellent, praiseworthy things of God.

Finally, brothers and sisters, whatever is true, whatever is noble, whatever is right, whatever is pure, whatever is lovely, whatever is admirable—if anything is excellent or praiseworthy—think about such things.

PHILIPPIANS 4:8 NIV

JUNE 20

When you have little kids, it can feel like being in constant survival mode. Survival mode by definition is short-lived—bodies can't sustain survival mode for a long time. When you're in survival mode, self-care can't happen in regular ways. There's simply no room for most kinds of self-care, except maybe a shower with the baby in a bouncy seat on the bathroom floor. Self-care looks different during different seasons of life, and that's okay. It doesn't have to be the same things forever but can continually shift to that which currently fills your soul. Those practices could be as simple as drinking more water, breathing deeper, taking a walk, or reading a book with our kids. Whatever looks like peace and rest to your soul—make space for these things. Jesus promises peace and rest. Let's take Him up on that offer.

Then Jesus said, "Come to Me, all of you who are weary and carry heavy burdens, and I will give you rest. Take My yoke upon you. Let Me teach you, because I am humble and gentle at heart, and you will find rest for your souls. For my yoke is easy to bear, and the burden I give you is light."

MATTHEW 11:28–30 NLT

JUNE 21

The young mother and her two toddlers show up at the garage sale. She chooses a few kitchen linens. And as she pays, her daughter picks up a stuffed bunny in a basket near the door. "We can't afford that, sweetie." The child seems to understand, and sets it down.

The homeowner pauses, then reaches down and hands the bunny to the girl. "You can have him, honey! I think he needs you to be his friend!"

Mercy costs very little to give but is a priceless gift to receive. Watch for ways you can hand that gift to those who don't deserve it. And when you do, you may just find it coming back around to you in unexpected ways.

Blessed are the merciful, for they shall receive mercy.
MATTHEW 5:7 NASB

JUNE 22

Milk, bread, diapers, new shoes…the list continues to grow. The physical needs of raising a family can feel overwhelming enough, but then there are the spiritual, emotional, and mental needs as well. You want your children to maintain balance, but it all seems like too much! Mom, are you feeling like you simply can't meet all the needs? It's because you can't. But the One you worship has promised to provide! God is your provider, and He is your family's provider as well. You can trust Him to keep His promises!

My God will supply all your needs according to His riches in glory in Christ Jesus.
PHILIPPIANS 4:19 HCSB

JUNE 23

What are you good at? Gymnastics? Meal planning? Spreadsheets? How do you feel about your parenting skills? Do they sometimes seem lacking?

Moses, the guy who led the Israelites out of slavery, received the Ten Commandments from God just after they escaped from Egypt. As Moses is explaining the commandments to the Israelites, he gives specific instructions on how to teach these commands to the children in the community.

Are you ready for this? He tells parents to sit, talk, walk, and lie down. We are all good at those things! These simple acts are perfect opportunities to talk to your children about God's laws.

Next time you are driving with your kids, playing outside, or getting them ready for bed and you think about the Lord and His Word, talk about it with your kids. It's the simplest way to parent with God's Word.

You shall teach them diligently to your children, and shall talk of them when you sit in your house, and when you walk by the way, and when you lie down, and when you rise.

DEUTERONOMY 6:7 ESV

JUNE 24

Love prevails when we forgive. When we hold on to a hurt, we hurt only ourselves. Love does not stay stuck on someone's fault, a focus that stops the flow of God's goodness in our lives. But when we focus on the forgiveness we both need and receive from Him, we see a clearer path to extend forgiveness to others. Forgive quickly, let love grow wildly, and watch your life become a field of beauty and blessing!

Love prospers when a fault is forgiven.
PROVERBS 17:9 NLT

JUNE 25

What if we spent more time in prayer throughout the day than we spent watching TV or scrolling through social media? What would it look like to really pray on every occasion? Prayer doesn't have to be a scheduled, sit-down occasion. Yes, it's good to have focused quiet time with God, but it's also a good practice to talk to Him as if He were hanging out with you while you go about your everyday life. (Because He is, you know.) It can be a driving-down-the-road, errand-running, laundry-folding, shower-taking kind of practice.

Prayer is simply an ongoing conversation with God, so go ahead and talk to Him about everything. When you don't know what to say, ask for the right words. When you don't know what to do, ask for the next step. When you are sad, ask for comfort. When you are glad, just praise Him!

Pray in the Spirit at all times and on every occasion.
EPHESIANS 6:18 NLT

JUNE 26

Mom tribes. Those tight-knit communities of mamas sharing the journey together. Having someone to call in a pinch, a save-the-day meal delivered, or a playdate that's fun for parents and kids—what could be better? Even if we're blessed with a circle of friends, it's good to remember that not everyone has found their niche. Some moms are flying solo, just doing what they can to stay afloat, maybe hoping for a connection but too afraid to ask. If we're already plugged in, let's keep our eyes and hearts open for those moms who aren't. And if we haven't found our place yet, that's okay too! Let's ask God to lead us. We're not called to make everyone a BFF, but we are called to love and care for one another. No one has to do this motherhood thing alone!

So in Christ we, though many, form one body, and each member belongs to all the others.

ROMANS 12:5 NIV

JUNE 27

We have all we need to bring God's love to the world…because we have Him! He's steady when our emotions aren't; He's patient when our patience is gone; and He sees the aching heart when all we see is the person in front of us. And maybe in the moment that person is hard to love. If that's the case, may we remember that God is all we need to respond to their love need…and His will is that we always do so.

I am with you; that is all you need.
II CORINTHIANS 12:9 TLB

JUNE 28

Think about the best mom you know. Maybe it's your own mom. Maybe it's a woman at church. What would she do to take care of you? Most likely, she would make sure you're comfortable. She'd get you a drink of water. Then she would advise you to take a bubble bath. Go to sleep. Turn off the TV, put down the phone, close the laptop. Invite a friend over. Laugh. Read a book. Eat food that nourishes your body—and also have dessert. Forgive yourself. Forgive another person. Hand over your worries to one who cares for you, and breathe deeply.

This is who God can be for us. This is one way God shows His care for us: like the best mother there ever was, ready to provide peace, relaxation, and maybe a little kick to get us going. Because sometimes moms need mothering too!

Give all your worries to God, for He cares about you.
I PETER 5:7 NLT

JUNE 29

There's an ache in your heart that has been there for quite some time. Maybe a change in circumstances prompted you to remember the hurt or a new situation aroused old feelings. And when you examine the ache a little deeper, you realize that while you said the words "I forgive you," you are harboring a bit of pain.

Though the wound is no longer new, now would be a beautiful time to soak in fresh forgiveness. Healing happens when you choose to offer grace and mercy. You've got this; the path to restoration and redemption is yours to be embraced.

Whenever you stand praying, forgive, if you have anything against anyone, so that your Father also who is in heaven may forgive you your trespasses.

MARK 11:25 ESV

JUNE 30

I love You, Father. That simple declaration of love is the best way to start any day. As we look to God with those words, we receive the strength and desire to love others better. We can't do it without Him. He's the Source of kindness, forgiveness, and patience, of all aspects of love. So may we who have been "called according to His purpose" love others with His love.

We know that all things work together for good to those who love God, to those who are the called according to His purpose.
ROMANS 8:28 NKJV

JULY 1

Moms know their kids. They know each birthmark, freckle, and crooked tooth. Moms can pick their kids out in a crowd, and their cries as babies are completely distinct to a mom. Moms know what will make kids laugh and when they're about to be reduced to tears. But most moms have never numbered their kids' hairs. That is an insurmountable task, and while we brush hair into braids and mohawks, we can remember that there is One who loves our kids even more.

God knows His plans for them. He knows every inch of their being, right down to the number of hairs on their heads. And each child matters even more to Him than they do to their mother (which is pretty incredible.) That's not just any ordinary kind of love; that's a love to be trusted.

What is the price of two sparrows—one copper coin? But not a single sparrow can fall to the ground without your Father knowing it. And the very hairs on your head are all numbered. So don't be afraid; you are more valuable to God than a whole flock of sparrows.

MATTHEW 10:29–31 NLT

JULY 2

You had been waiting for the phone call for what seemed like an eternity, and finally, finally, it came! But as you listened to the voice on the other side, disappointment flooded your heart. The news was not what you were expecting to hear.

Recovering from life's letdowns can be tough. You wonder how to move forward. But the Lord loves you and longs to use all things for your good. Especially through disappointments, He wants you to know that He never stops loving you.

This I call to mind, and therefore I have hope: The steadfast love of the LORD never ceases; his mercies never come to an end.
LAMENTATIONS 3:21–22 ESV

JULY 3

Think about it. How can we do anything with the fullness of God's presence when we have worry taking up space in our hearts and minds? May we release those worries and embrace both the fullness of His presence and the joy it brings. Such joyfulness is a loving thing to bring into the world. We need more of it! Let's give God our cares, worries, and woes and walk with joy today no matter what does or doesn't go our way!

Let Him have all your worries and cares,
for He is always thinking about you.
I PETER 5:7 TLB

JULY 4

You can't go to a toy store or a park without seeing a little girl with a tiara on her head. She's probably got on some sparkly plastic earrings and a tutu to round out her royalty.

Did you know Jesus offers some princess-y type gifts to us? He has promised us a crown of beauty, oil of joy, and a garment of praise! He wants to give us these items in trade.

We give Him our ashes. You know, ashes of a dead relationship or dream? He trades us a crown of beauty. We give Him our mourning. He pours on a soothing oil of joy. We give up our spirit of despair. He clothes us in a garment of praise. Take Jesus up on these trades! Don't stay in your darkness; turn to the King of kings so He can clothe you, His princess!

The Spirit of the LORD GOD is on Me, because the LORD has anointed Me... to give them a crown of beauty instead of ashes, festive oil instead of mourning, and splendid clothes instead of despair.

ISAIAH 61:1, 3 HCSB

JULY 5

As mothers, we have to try really hard NOT to worry, especially about the future. Some of us worry about the little things of tomorrow like who will sit by our kids during lunch at their new school. Some of us worry about the bigger things of tomorrow like how we are going to pay for college. But regardless of what we're worrying about, what does it actually achieve for us? Nothing at all!

Worrying about tomorrow won't change the outcome of the situation, but it will rob us of our joy today. It takes up valuable real estate in our hearts and minds, and prevents us from being present with others. So let's turn our worry over to our ever-capable God. Doing so demonstrates our trust in Him, and it frees up our thoughts and emotions to handle whatever this day will bring.

So don't worry about tomorrow, for tomorrow will bring its own worries. Today's trouble is enough for today.
MATTHEW 6:34 NLT

JULY 6

Let your faith ignite your dreams. If your hope is in Christ, it's on a course to come true. Your dream is tied to your gift, and every gift you have came from Him. Time is simply God preparing your heart for more than you dared to imagine.

Now we have a far better hope, for Christ makes us acceptable to God, and now we may draw near to Him.
HEBREWS 7:19 TLB

JULY 7

Motherhood is busy! Working, playing, cooking, cleaning, comforting, cheering, chauffeuring…the list goes on. We moms have needs, too—little ones and big ones—all day long. And we have a choice about how to meet those needs. When something unexpected happens, someone gets hurt, something is lost, someone is late, where do we go first? To the Word or to the world? Matthew 7:7 says: "Ask and it will be given to you; seek and you will find; knock and the door will be opened to you" (NIV). We may apply this truth to the big things in life, but it's important to remember that nothing's too small for God's loving care. Lost keys? Hurt feelings? Chaotic morning? Let's take a moment and remember His promises. Post them around the house if we have to! Whatever it takes to help us breathe a little easier and live a little freer every day.

My God will supply all your needs according to His riches in glory in Christ Jesus.

PHILIPPIANS 4:19 NASB

JULY 8

Pinterest can be irresistible when planning a birthday party. Pages and pages of themed wonderlands, DIY treats and crafts, and ideas for making a special day complete perfection. But when the laptop closes and reality snaps back into focus, real life can look less than fantastic. Here's the thing: your kids won't remember perfect birthday parties, but they will remember if their mom was a train wreck during those parties. As a memory maker, moms don't have to try to make the days perfect—we only need to find the beauty in our real life, and make sure our kids see and experience it too. *That* is where their stories will come from. Give your kids memories of a lifetime spent treasure hunting for eternal beauty.

God has made everything beautiful for its own time. He has planted eternity in the human heart.
ECCLESIASTES 3:11 NLT

JULY 9

Created in God's image, yet we're all so distinctly different. You are incredibly special; do you think about that often enough? No one else on earth takes the same path you do, but God makes sure you cross paths with exactly the right people—the ones meant to be in your story. Love the souls in your story today…and give a little of God's love to the ones who pass through.

Thank You for making me so wonderfully complex! It is amazing to think about.
PSALM 139:14 TLB

JULY 10

Late again! No way! But yes, here you are, rushing out the door with two kids and a dog in tow, trying to make the school drop-off time and keep the vet appointment too. Amid the rush, you pass someone who needs help. A small sign catches your eye and you know that stopping to give him your lunch is what you are supposed to do. You can pack another lunch when you return the puppy home. "Thank You, Lord, for prompting my heart to obey Your Spirit."

This is how we have come to know love: He laid down His life for us. We should also lay down our lives for our brothers.
I JOHN 3:16 HCSB

JULY 11

Stuffy. Stodgy. Old-fashioned. Some people think the Bible is best used as a history book. It might even be a book worth studying for the beautiful poetry and moral stories.

As Christians, we know the Bible isn't just words on a page. The Bible is God's Word. God's words are alive. He inspired the writers of those sixty-six books to write these living words so we could know, love, and even use His words. There are situations where we need supernatural instruction, insight, and power that only God's Word can give. When we go to God's Word and ask God to show us the living Word that brings life, He will. When we wield His Word like a sword, by speaking it and praying it, we will see miracles happen in our lives!

For the word of God is alive and active. Sharper than any double-edged sword, it penetrates even to dividing soul and spirit, joints and marrow; it judges the thoughts and attitudes of the heart.

HEBREWS 4:12 NIV

JULY 12

God's faithfulness is in every sunrise, every moment, and every season. Our days come and go by what His heart plans and His hand guides. Not one of the days He gives should be lived with fear of failure. What might look like a mess to us will become a part of the masterpiece He's making of our lives in Him.

We are God's masterpiece. He has created us anew in Christ Jesus, so we can do the good things He planned for us long ago.
EPHESIANS 2:10 NLT

JULY 13

I've got that joy-joy-joy-joy down in my heart! WHERE? Down in my heart! WHERE? Down in my heart! I've got that joy-joy-joy-joy down in my heart! Down in my heart to stay!

Sometimes the songs you learned as a kid stick with you long after you've grown up, and then one day you begin singing them to your kids. Here's an interesting phenomenon: the same simple words you sang at the top of your lungs in the front pew at VBS take on a totally different and deeper meaning now that you're an adult. Let's face it. Joy is harder to find when you are adulting than it was when you were a carefree child at play. But what if it wasn't? Perhaps being full of joy-joy-joy-joy is as simple as Psalm 128:1 says it is—by fearing the Lord and following His ways!

How joyful are those who fear the
Lord—all who follow His ways!
PSALM 128:1 NLT

JULY 14

Naps. Why in the world can't toddlers understand how amazing they are? Even as their little eyelids flutter closed, some kids do everything they can to stay awake. And even when they fuss, we insist they lie down because we know what their growing bodies need. In the same way, our spirits can become weary, and we, too, can ignore the signs. A sense of restlessness, emptiness, or doubt creeps in, and before we realize it, we're in a rut wondering how in the world we got there. The Lord knows long before we do that we're going to need a recharge. He sees the path ahead and offers the refreshment our hearts need. As we learn to listen for His still, small voice calling us to rest, we'll move more and more from surviving to thriving in every area of our lives.

I came that they may have life
and have it abundantly.
JOHN 10:10 ESV

JULY 15

Let God's favor shine on us today, His grace bringing so much good that our hearts gush with gratefulness. How can that not-of-this-world love be in us and not inspire us to take every step with joy and touch every life with kindness? Make the moments mindful of giving: all that we can of Him for all that He's done for us.

Let Your favor shine on Your servant.
PSALM 31:16 NLT

JULY 16

Kids loves puzzles. Not all moms love puzzles in large part because of all the pieces (pieces are a mom's nemesis) and because of the missing pieces. At the end of every puzzle there's usually a hole, the result of a piece gone missing. It's the worst!

We all belong to a larger body, and our stories are pieces of a big puzzle. When our stories go untold, a piece of the puzzle is lost. We need to tell our stories—even the regular, everyday, real life, mundane stories—to both find ourselves in the bigger picture and to make space for one another. In the big picture of the full body, you're right where He wants you to be. Put together the whole puzzle. Tell your story.

God has placed the parts in the body, every one of them, just as He wanted them to be.
1 CORINTHIANS 12:18 NIV

JULY 17

You woke up with a headache and it's your week to serve at church. All you want to do is crawl back into bed, but something is prompting you to hop into the shower. After taking some pain meds, you determine to fulfill your commitment. And the sweetest elderly lady stops you in the hallway.

"Honey, I see you every week here and I just want you to know that you make me smile."

"Well, you make me smile!"

And your heart swells with joy; by now you've forgotten that you ever had a headache.

Therefore, my dear brothers, be steadfast, immovable, always excelling in the Lord's work, knowing that your labor in the Lord is not in vain.
I CORINTHIANS 15:58 HCSB

JULY 18

By grace alone we press on, find peace, and move forward. It's the hardest thing to do sometimes, to forget what hurt us so badly. But that's what grace is so good at—helping us see that forgiveness is for all people and all things, no matter how fierce the wound or how far the fall.

Continue to rely on the grace of God.
ACTS 13:43 NLT

JULY 19

"Get down! Stop doing that! Come over here now! Not in your mouth! Quiet! Stand still! Be careful! Where do dirty dishes go?!" How many times have those words been out of your mouth... today? As moms, we have a whole repertoire of words and phrases to use for correcting our kids. Some phrases work better than others. The best words we can use? God's words. Scripture is full of instruction for us and is perfect to use in teaching our children to know God's way of living. We can use Scripture to rebuke our children because we know it's correct, and not our own fleshly desire to see our kids act "right." When we use God's Word as a measuring stick for attitudes, behavior, and interaction with others, we are training our children not in being little examples of our parenting skills, but in the righteousness of God.

All Scripture is God-breathed and is useful for teaching, rebuking, correcting and training in righteousness.
II TIMOTHY 3:16 NIV

JULY 20

When our kids were born, God didn't gift us with an indexed instruction manual full of wisdom on how to raise them. That would have been dreamy, but we would have missed out on a critical part of the parenting process: reliance on Him. He gave mothers a big job to do, but He didn't give us all the wisdom we needed right off the bat. (We probably couldn't have handled it if He did.) He strategically created us to need Him, and the beauty of it all is that the only way to get what we need from Him is to get close to Him. It requires a relationship. Isn't that brilliant? The Lord has all the wisdom we need, and He promises to share it with us generously if we just ask. Are you ready to receive it?

If any of you lacks wisdom, let him ask God, who gives generously to all without reproach, and it will be given him.
JAMES 1:5 ESV

JULY 21

God is the heart's refuge and the soul's courage. In everything that tests our faith and hope today, God is our tested and trustworthy help. He will not fail us if we call on Him, because He's called into action by His unfailing love—and no power on earth or beyond can slow it or stop it from reaching us.

God is our refuge and strength, a
tested help in times of trouble.
PSALM 46:1 TLB

JULY 22

Have you noticed how terribly thirsty kids become at bedtime? Or how suddenly they ask for all the stories? All the hugs? During the day, it can be hard to slow them down for anything! But when the sun sets and the world darkens, they seem to need us again and again. We know it's not the tenth drink of water they really crave; it's the assurance of our presence. They just want to know we are near. And we grown-ups are not so different. When times of darkness fall in our lives, we reach out for our Father. No request is too great or too small in His eyes. He never tires of us; He knows our need, even before we can articulate it. Like the most patient, gentle, loving parent, He reminds us again and again: Do not be afraid. I'm here. You are safe in the warmth of My love.

I will never leave you nor forsake you.
HEBREWS 13:5 ESV

JULY 23

Sometimes the monotony of motherhood is exhausting. The days blur together in a fog of crumbs, carpool, homework, practice, appointments, and laundry. The same motions, day after day—how can they possibly matter? The beginnings are too small to make a difference. But they are not too small. Nothing is too small for God to make glorious. Even in the goldfish crumbs, the minivan full of everything except a spare diaper, and the mac & cheese meals—even in these "ordinary" things and small beginnings, extraordinary is present because He is there. He is there in the big, the little, and in all the parts of our lives, and that matters.

Do not despise these small beginnings, for the LORD rejoices to see the work begin.
ZECHARIAH 4:10 NLT

JULY 24

God's got you today—on the solid ground of His love and the steady path of your purpose. Nothing that happens is going to destroy the good things He has planned for you. If there's a detour, He's already seen it and made a way around it. If you slip, He's there to catch you. Take your steps with confidence. God's in control of each one.

He set my feet on solid ground and steadied me as I walked along.
PSALM 40:2 NLT

JULY 25

"I want that!" "No, it's mine." And there they are, arguing again. It feels like you should have rented a referee shirt to handle sibling rivalry. While you're tempted to walk away and let them settle it their own way, you know that peacemaking is pivotal for your home and family. The peace of God is higher than you can comprehend, and it transcends above all. Yes, even sibling rivalry.

Take a moment to ask the Lord to fill you with His peace and embrace the future rewards your children will own as they learn to become peacemakers.

Peacemakers who sow in peace reap
a harvest of righteousness.
JAMES 3:18 NIV

JULY 26

Has it been a bad day? Did your kids stomp all over you? Did your husband hurt your feelings? Or did something worse happen—the loss of a friend? A family member? A dream?

Does your heart feel broken in a million pieces? Broken hearts are very lonely. No one can seem to understand what it's like to be alone with the devastating news, situation, or feelings.

No one, except our God. He promises to be close to you when you are brokenhearted. What a relief! When everyone else moves away, unsure of what to do about your pain, you can be sure that God is close to you. He moves in on your broken heart and crushed spirit. He can hold you, carry you, love you, and save you in times of the worst pain!

The LORD is near the brokenhearted;
He saves those crushed in spirit.
PSALM 34:18 HCSB

JULY 27

In every single moment of your life, God is orchestrating what is best for your well-being. Be well today! Lean into love, look for the need, and seek the good of those around you. God will turn your kind words and loving actions into blessings—so be ready for the pure joy that love brings, because God is going to give it!

Let no one seek his own, but each one the other's well-being.
I CORINTHIANS 10:24 NKJV

JULY 28

New strength for a new day—that's a promise to believe and be thankful for. We don't always have leftover courage to carry us if there have been too many days of fighting hard to believe and crying tears of disappointment and holding on with slipping hands. But God knew when He created us that we'd need new hope daily. So here it is: all the hope and strength you need today, straight from His almighty hand.

Your strength shall be renewed day by day like morning dew.
PSALM 110:3 TLB

JULY 29

Relationships are messy, because people are messy. The hardest days are when we let our differences divide us, instead of letting our similarities unite us. Yet God calls us to live in complete harmony with each other. Complete harmony? Is that even possible? What does that look like in real life, especially with the people in our own homes? We've all had glimpses of it, but how do we live our lives so it's more of the norm than not? There's not a secret formula, but these things are for sure: we can't be selfish, we can't slack off, and we have to stick close to God. He promises to refill us with patience and encouragement and to help us when we need it. Let's practice these behaviors in our own homes, so we are ready as believers to live in complete harmony with each other everywhere we go.

May God, who gives this patience and encouragement, help you live in complete harmony with each other, as is fitting for followers of Christ Jesus.
ROMANS 15:5 NLT

JULY 30

That pile. We all know the one. It sits on the front table, or that desk no one uses. Might stare at us from the kitchen counter as we sip our morning coffee. It's school forms, party invitations, kid creations, half-written thank-you notes—maybe a few things we don't even recognize anymore. When we see it, we're reminded of the million things to do today (or someday!), and sometimes it just feels like too much, all at once. But our heavenly Father? He doesn't see a big mess—on our counters or in our lives. He sees every detail, knows every need, and promises His peace in the midst of it all. Best of all, He sees His daughters, doing our best, doing what we can, when we can, however we can. And He loves us just as we are. Let's let go of striving today and receive His grace and guidance for every little thing.

My God shall supply all your need according to His riches in glory by Christ Jesus.
PHILIPPIANS 4:19 NKJV

JULY 31

It can't be taken from you or broken through. God's armor isn't made on earth, but it can shield our hearts from the darkness here. He gives comfort to the grieving and hope to the hurting. He gives joy to the discouraged and strength to the fearful. And the greatest barrier we have in any battle is the power of His love for us.

His faithful promises are your armor.
PSALM 91:4 TLB

AUGUST 1

Has it been one of those days? Are you feeling defeated, defensive, and alone? Have you said something you regret? Are the kids running amok? And is it only 9 a.m.?

Take a breath. You are doing a fantastic job. God has loved you with an everlasting love, and you are showing that kind of love to your kids. No matter how much daylight is left today, know deep down that you are enough because God is enough in you. Your kids see more of God because of the love you pour into them. And isn't loving them the real job anyway? At the end of the day, if the only things you've accomplished are having kept the kids away from permanent markers, fed them and yourself, and given them a bunch of hugs, then, Mama, you did it. You did it, and you are loved (and loving) unfailingly.

Long ago the LORD said to Israel: "I have loved you, My people, with an everlasting love. With unfailing love, I have drawn you to Myself."
JEREMIAH 31:3 NLT

AUGUST 2

Another busy day and mentally, you are working your way through dinner, cleanup, homework, and all the other steps that lead children to their beds. Frankly you just want to sit down for a few moments to rest; this thought is threatening to wreak havoc in your brain because of all the things you know you need to do before that. But the Lord knows all that you need to do. And His perfect peace is there for you when you trust His plan and His timing.

You will keep in perfect peace those whose minds are steadfast, because they trust in You.
ISAIAH 26:3 NIV

AUGUST 3

Our hearts are going to need some never-give-up on the way to our dreams. God sees them and He'll be faithful to see them through; we just need to trust and surrender to His timing. The greatest part of His timing? It's always in line with His best.

A desire accomplished is sweet to the soul.
PROVERBS 13:19 NKJV

AUGUST 4

Do you know King Asa? He was king of Judah soon after King David. He was a strong man of God who tore down idols and encouraged all of Judah to worship God. One day, a large army came against him. Asa marched out to meet them, and his army took their positions.

But before they began to fight, Asa prayed, "Lord, there is no one like You to help the powerless against the mighty. Help us, Lord our God, for we rely on You, and in Your name we have come against this vast army." What a strong prayer! There is no question, no doubt of God's power, ability, or desire to help. And help God did. God struck down the army while Asa and his men carried off the plunder!

Next time an enemy is in your way, pray like Asa. Rely on God and His power!

LORD, there is no one besides You to help the mighty and those without strength. Help us, LORD our God, for we depend on You, and in Your name we have come against this large army. Yahweh, You are our God. Do not let a mere mortal hinder You.

II CHRONICLES 14:11 HCSB

AUGUST 5

There is potentially nothing more frustrating as a parent than telling your kids what you expect of them and then watching them do nothing—or even worse, the exact opposite. We shake our heads in disbelief at their disobedience, but are we really that different when it comes to obeying our heavenly Father? Do we always have a good attitude about what He's asking of us and obey perfectly without delay? Not hardly. But aren't we thankful for God's patience with us and His grace for second chances? We can even be grateful for the consequences, because they produce obedience too. Make this real for your kids by sharing an example of your desire to obey God but your struggle in walking it out. Remind them that God expects obedience from all of His children, no matter how old they are. When they obey you, they are obeying God too.

Children, obey your parents as you would the Lord, because this is right.
EPHESIANS 6:1 HCSB

AUGUST 6

You are loved perfectly, forgiven completely, and cared for constantly. God won't quit you. When it feels like a lonely journey at times, this life in Him, know that He quietly carries you forward to the purposes up ahead—and they are always good.

I will be your God through all your lifetime,
yes, even when your hair is white with age.
I made you and I will care for you. I will
carry you along and be your Savior.
ISAIAH 46:4 TLB

AUGUST 7

Even the most beautiful places in the world can be ruined by a polluted atmosphere. And our homes are no exception. We may have the loveliest décor and the latest everything, but when bitterness, grumbling, stress, or strife sets in, ugliness prevails. God's Word is full of ways to bring His beauty into our everyday lives—choosing joy, speaking the truth in love, building up instead of tearing down… If we truly desire His kingdom life to fill our homes, we must first allow it to fill our hearts—all of our hearts.

Can we sit with our families and share ideas for clearing the air? For allowing more goodness, grace, and truth to brighten our days together? Let's ask our kids how they perceive our home life and what ideas they might have for making Jesus a more welcome guest. We may be surprised at how simple some changes can be!

My people will live in peaceful dwelling places,
in secure homes, in undisturbed places of rest.
ISAIAH 32:18 NIV

AUGUST 8

Kids ask a thousand questions every day. "When is lunch? Can we have a snack? Where is my bear? Can you drive me to a friend's house? Why?" It can be easy to start drowning out their questions, letting them melt into the background noise and not really hearing their requests. Isn't it wonderful news that God always hears our prayers? He hears the everyday chatter. He hears the impassioned, pleading, and tear-filled prayers. He hears the muttered-under-your-breath pleas for patience. He hears the silent moments when the Spirit intercedes for us. He hears the joyful praises. God hears them all. Not one word is overlooked. May you feel the peace of knowing that each word spoken to the Lord is delivered.

This is the confidence we have in approaching God: that if we ask anything according to His will, He hears us. And if we know that He hears us—whatever we ask—we know that we have what we asked of Him.

I JOHN 5:14–15 NIV

AUGUST 9

A new day begins, and God's love draws us in. Not by fear or force but by loving us first and fully. There are no empty places in the vastness of His love—like the sky above and the air around. Let it fill you and hold you and heal you. And know it will never leave you.

I have loved you...with an everlasting love. With unfailing love I have drawn you to Myself.
JEREMIAH 31:3 NLT

AUGUST 10

Which school should she attend? Where should you go to church now? What will happen if you must move across town? The questions keep coming and the answers weigh heavily on you. It's okay, Mama! The One who loves your soul longs to be your guide. He is not leaving you to make the decisions all on your own. For as long as eternity, God will help you take another step and then another. So, take a deep breath and ask Him to show you the way.

For this God is our God for ever and ever;
He will be our guide even to the end.
PSALM 48:14 NIV

AUGUST 11

There is a story in the book of Acts about a woman named Lydia. She was near the river with other women, perhaps washing clothes or selling the purple cloth she was known for, when Paul and Silas approached and began to teach about Jesus. Lydia believed Paul's message. She and her family were baptized and she asked Paul and Silas to stay at her house.

Later, Paul and Silas were arrested, imprisoned, and set free (by God!) and went straight to Lydia's house afterward. In only four short verses, we learn so much from this strong lady. Lydia was quick to believe and act on God's words. (Without research?) Lydia offered hospitality right away. (Without even making sure her house was clean?) She got involved with the church immediately. (Without checking her schedule?!) Let's be like Lydia and rush into serving, loving, and believing the Lord!

If you consider me a believer in the Lord, come and stay at my house.
ACTS 16:15 HCSB

AUGUST 12

Whatever God has for your hands to do today, put your heart into it too. Give it to God, and give it your all. There won't be a single regret in the moments you choose to serve Him. Love will be in them, patience will prevail, and somewhere in there a heart will be blessed because you're being a blessing.

Give generously...not grudgingly, for the L*ORD* *your God will bless you in everything you do.*
DEUTERONOMY 15:10 NLT

AUGUST 13

Remember how much trust it took to leave your firstborn in someone else's care for the very first time? The way you choked back the tears as you walked out the door, thought about them the whole time you were gone, and kept your phone nearby just in case? Raising children can be an overwhelming responsibility, but we can trust God to make provision for it all.

Parenting is an ongoing journey of learning to trust yourself, trust your kids, and trust others. Beyond that, it is a personal and proactive process of learning to trust the Lord with all your heart—especially when you don't understand. If you are at a loss with your kids, you can trust Him to show you the way. His paths are straight. His will is right. His love is strong. Is there a better place for a mother to be?

Trust in the LORD *with all your heart; do not depend on your own understanding. Seek His will in all you do, and He will show you which path to take.*

PROVERBS 3:5–6 NLT

AUGUST 14

For most of us, procrastination is an uninvited guest in our lives. Yet it always finds a way to pull up a chair and make itself at home. Maybe it's work deadlines, home organization, returning messages, filling out forms… Whatever we didn't get unloaded yesterday feels twice as heavy today. And we don't even want to think about tomorrow!

There may be some great tips out there on how to stop putting things off, but there's one simple thing we can all give ourselves right now: grace. Unless we're robots, it's unlikely that we'll have things done 100 percent right, and right on time, every time. Eventually we all drop a ball (or ten). If we're buried right now, let's ask the Lord to help us check a few things off, and maybe even let a few things go. Remember: the world isn't waiting to be saved by our to-do lists—and (thank heaven!) neither are we.

From his fullness we have all received, grace upon grace.
JOHN 1:16 ESV

AUGUST 15

No measurement on earth can determine the riches God gives, and our hearts can't fully contain them. That's how it is with eternal things, God things. There isn't a single material aspect about them, but they materialize in abundant, full, and everlasting life. It's amazing to think it's as simple as asking, but it is. Ask Him for what your heart needs today—and open it wide for the overflow.

All have the same Lord who generously gives His riches to all those who ask Him for them.
ROMANS 10:12 TLB

AUGUST 16

Being a mom is wearying, and it can be easy to let tempers—and words—fly. The tongue is an incredibly powerful thing. With it we can change lives for the better, or for the worse. We can bless, or we can curse. We can steer toward love, or toward destruction. It's a hard thing to control. But if we can tame our tongues, we will reap benefits a hundredfold. A calmer countenance. More trusting relationships with our families. A more peaceful home. It's worth the often-extraordinary effort to take a deep breath and steer our ship in the direction of love.

We can make a large horse go wherever we want by means of a small bit in its mouth. And a small rudder makes a huge ship turn wherever the pilot chooses to go, even though the winds are strong. In the same way, the tongue is a small thing that makes grand speeches. But a tiny spark can set a great forest on fire.

JAMES 3:3–5 NLT

AUGUST 17

"Thank you." Her simple words made your heart swell for her sincere gratefulness. How thoughtful to have your simple act recognized and appreciated!

To give thanks is to show the status of one's heart. Have you taken a moment recently to give God thanks for His work in your life? Perhaps the friend He sent your way yesterday or the coffee you drank this morning is an everyday reason to give thanks.

"Father, thank You for providing for me and for loving me so much. My heart is grateful for who You are."

Enter His gates with thanksgiving and His courts with praise. Give thanks to Him and praise His name.
PSALM 100:4 HCSB

AUGUST 18

Stand in the unwavering confidence that you can do anything God calls you to do today, and believe it will be blessed. His light in you is now a beacon for others who are searching…hoping…hurting. Shine the goodness of the One who called you and saved you, who carries you and cares for you—and let His love keep lighting the world.

You can show others the goodness of God, for He called you out of the darkness into His wonderful light.
I PETER 2:9 NLT

AUGUST 19

Searching for new recipes online is a bottomless hole. You can get lost for hours searching for the perfect meal for your family. The Internet is just full of perfectly positioned foods that really do look good enough to eat!

Jesus tells His followers that if anyone gives even a cup of cold water (not a fancy meal) to a child who follows Him, that person will receive a reward. It's not clear what the reward is, but wouldn't you like to receive a reward from Jesus? And how much more tremendous would that reward be if you offered Living Water to your children? If you told your children about Jesus and His plans and purposes for them, what would that reward be?

Just as we plan and pore over recipes, let's do the same with presenting Jesus to our children! You will be rewarded!

And if anyone gives even a cup of cold water to one of these little ones who is My disciple, truly I tell you, that person will certainly not lose their reward.
MATTHEW 10:42 NIV

AUGUST 20

Remember the last time you had an idea, made a plan, worked hard, and made something you were proud of? Maybe you baked a fancy birthday cake for a friend. Maybe you sewed an Easter dress for your daughter. Maybe you made a wreath for your front door. Maybe you planted a garden in your backyard. Whatever you created, remember how you felt when you were finally finished? Wasn't it rewarding to sit back, relax, and delight in what you made? Imagine God doing the same thing with you! He had the good idea of you, made a plan to create you, picked your parents for you, and gave you a birthday. How He must have delighted in you the day you were born—a proud Father admiring what He made, and calling you very good!

God saw all that He had made, and it was very good.
GENESIS 1:31 HCSB

AUGUST 21

Be blessed with a quiet heart today. God is taking care of everything, including our moments. They come and go so quickly, but if we invite Him into all of them, they add up to a whole lot of love in a day. And isn't that what makes our lives more memorable: more and more and more love? May you know how much He loves you, right now and always, and may that knowledge fill your heart with hope.

Lord, when doubts fill my mind, when
my heart is in turmoil, quiet me and
give me renewed hope and cheer.
PSALM 94:19 TLB

AUGUST 22

It goes so fast. Don't blink. Cherish the moments. How many times has someone shared this well-meaning wisdom? We know it's true, and we do savor the blessings of daily life with our kids—but some days are tough. Some nights we count the minutes before bedtime because we're spent. We've left it all out on the field and we Just. Need. A. Break.

Ever beat yourself up for getting a little frazzled? It's good to remember that running low doesn't mean there's something wrong. We may simply need a refill. God didn't design us to run on empty; He designed us to need Him in every way. Let's remember this as we fall into bed after a long day. There's always one thing left on our list: rest in Him.

Then Jesus said, "Let's go off by ourselves to a quiet place and rest awhile."
MARK 6:31 NLT

AUGUST 23

Scrolling through Instagram, there are beautiful kitchens. Vases full of fresh flowers, sunlight streaming through sparkling windows, and bowls full of apples on the counter. When we lower our phones and glance at our own kitchen, we may see dishes piled in the sink, half-eaten bananas on the counter, and the dog licking crumbs off the floor. Not exactly Insta-worthy. But if we snapped a picture, it would reflect the state of our real life and our hearts, capturing us right in the middle of choosing our kids. Patiently helping with homework instead of scrubbing the sink and doing the dishes. Sitting on the floor and playing cars. Talking and laughing over cookies (hence the crumbs) and glasses of milk.

A clean sink would be great, but today let's choose connection over cleaning. The dishes will wait, but our kids' hearts? Those won't.

As water reflects the face, so the heart reflects the person.
PROVERBS 27:19 HCSB

AUGUST 24

A peaceful heart in a noisy world and a busy life—we're going to need to lean into God for that today. He loves us and heals us inside and out, and staying calm in the chaos keeps our hearts well. There isn't a thing we can do to change the things only He can, so we'll just trust Him moment by moment and cling to His peace through it all.

A peaceful heart leads to a healthy body.
PROVERBS 14:30 NLT

AUGUST 25

You read another news story and it brings the reality of the world today to the forefront. Tragedies of all kinds easily shake you and cause you to forget that the Lord is watching over you. His strength will hold you when you are afraid. His protection covers all circumstances and situations. When terror threatens to strike you and you are afraid of harm, remember that the Lord is faithful to provide strength and protection every moment of every day. Not only when you feel you need it, but even when you don't know that you need it! That's God's promise.

The Lord is faithful; He will strengthen and guard you from the evil one.
II THESSALONIANS 3:3 HCSB

AUGUST 26

Building a house is painstaking. You have to choose each individual knob, paint color, and type of light bulb. However, when you're done, you have a home to protect you, shield you, and gather your family. As much as we want our homes to have all the shiplap and cozy decor, God says that a real house is built through wisdom. He tells us that a house is established with understanding. And if we want to fill our home with treasures, it will take knowledge.

It sounds like building a house, or rather managing a home, taking care of children, and becoming a wife of noble character, begins not with a foundation and a construction crew but with me. Cry out to God for wisdom, understanding, and knowledge. Just as you'd pick out the specifics of baseboards and chandeliers, spend time looking in God's Word for wisdom from Him.

A house is built by wisdom, and it is established by understanding; by knowledge the rooms are filled with every precious and beautiful treasure.

PROVERBS 24:3–4 HCSB

AUGUST 27

God guides all your moments with love, and all your moments are leading to good things. Trusting Him will not disappoint, and loving Him will satisfy every need. Today is one step closer to the things your heart desires—and strength in you that you've never known before.

The Lord will guide you continually, and satisfy you with all good things.
ISAIAH 58:11 TLB

AUGUST 28

God created mothers with hearts that care deeply for their children. We concern ourselves regularly with things like their well-being, their safety, their future, and their faith. These and many other things weigh heavily on our minds and can end up taking up residence in our hearts. That's not a surprise to God. He knew we would overthink and analyze and feel all the feels, yet He never meant for us to carry our concerns alone. God cares about us in a way that only a kindhearted heavenly Father can. He is ready and able to handle anything we send His way or drop off at the foot of the cross. We can lighten our minds and our hearts if we simply hand our cares over to Him. He is waiting for us to do so.

Give all your worries and cares to
God, for He cares about you.
I PETER 5:7 NLT

AUGUST 29

Family road trips. We always begin with high hopes: Snacks ready. Art supplies. Maybe a DVD. But a few hours in, things may start going south. Drinks spill. Crayons break. "We've seen this movie a thousand times, Mom! When will we get there!?"

We give the kids a hard time, but it happens to us too. A few moments of life's discomforts—unwanted feelings or experiences—and we may begin to wish we were anywhere but here. We check out, dream about the future, and forget that we can never have these hours back. Jesus always calls us back to the moment. Back to being grateful. Back to choosing joy where we are and loving who we're with.

Next time we find ourselves in one of life's road-trip moments, let's take a breath and come back to the present. We never know what blessings might be waiting there.

I have learned the secret of being content—whether well fed or hungry, whether in abundance or in need. I am able to do all things through Him who strengthens me.

PHILIPPIANS 4:12–13 HCSB

AUGUST 30

If we want to be truly happy, we have to keep our focus on love—God's love for us and God's love through us. We weren't created to go it alone, and since we need each other, we need to help each other. Let's do some things today in the spirit of love…and get ready to have a happy heart.

Fill all who love You with Your happiness.
PSALM 5:11 TLB

AUGUST 31

Moms are the glue. Moms are the ones who hold families together, who create traditions, who remember the details. Moms are the ones who send back permission slips, bring cookies for the preschool party, and add entries to the calendar. At least, as moms we may feel like we're expected to do all these things. But what if the expectations were scrapped, and love, joy, and peace were embraced instead? What if God's expectations mattered more than what the world says we have to produce in order to be successful?

Let God be the glue. Let Him hold together the details of your life. And fill your head and heart with Scripture, pulling up verses as comfort, inspiration, and truth. Success will come when your life unfolds from those verses stored up in your heart.

This book of instruction must not depart from your mouth; you are to recite it day and night so that you may carefully observe everything written in it. For then you will prosper and succeed in whatever you do.

JOSHUA 1:8 HCSB

SEPTEMBER 1

His personality shines and you ponder how differently he interacts with others than you do. Yes, he's your son; but oh, it's so hard to think like he is thinking. Did God choose the wrong parent for the job? Nope. You were expertly and divinely chosen as his mom. There is no reason to feel insecure in the role God has called you to fulfill in his life. He will equip you to walk through it. He is all you need to sustain you and secure you in this parenting position.

"Thank You, Lord, for secure steps to parenting well!"

Lord, You are my portion and my cup of blessing; You hold my future.
PSALM 16:5 HCSB

SEPTEMBER 2

Some rest in the goodness of God sounds like a great plan for the day. Even if it gets a little crazy on the outside, there's a quiet on the inside that can't be shaken. It's anchored in the One who's anchored our souls in everlasting hope. He's been good to us and He'll be good to us—and that will never change.

Let my soul be at rest again, for the
LORD has been good to me.
PSALM 116:7 NLT

SEPTEMBER 3

There are days we all want to hide from life. We want to curl up on the couch, tight-lipped, disdainful, sullen, and selfish. We feel vindicated when we hide our pain in food, YouTube, fiction, pride, anger, or busyness. But we know hiding in those places can't last forever and only draws us deeper into ourselves. God offers a better choice. We can hide ourselves in Him.

When we see our enemies looming—fear, selfishness, discontent, aggravation, self-pity, and more—we can run to Him and hide there. Hide in God! What a comforting thought, to be hidden in and by Him. In that beautiful hiding place we will discover God as leader, rescuer, teacher, and protector. He is waiting for you to hide in Him, seeking you to hide.

Rescue me from my enemies, Lord,
for I hide myself in You.
PSALM 143:9 NIV

SEPTEMBER 4

Disagreements are a real part of being in authentic relationship with others, especially within families. How do we love others well in the midst of conflict? How can we prioritize the other person so we can preserve the relationship? Is it possible to manage our emotions so anger doesn't turn into sin? Yes. God gives us a three-step strategy for engaging with those we disagree with in a Christlike manner: be quick to listen, slow to speak, and slow to get angry. We will be good listeners if we are slow to speak. We will be slow to speak if we are being a good listener. If we have done the first two steps well, then we will automatically be slow to get angry.

Understand this, my dear brothers and sisters: You must all be quick to listen, slow to speak, and slow to get angry.
JAMES 1:19 NLT

SEPTEMBER 5

If we could see the blessings God has prepared for us, we'd see that what we're walking through now is preparing our hearts to receive them. We don't want what our hearts aren't ready for—and no one knows our hearts better than the One who created them.

There shall be showers, showers of blessing.
EZEKIEL 34:26 TLB

SEPTEMBER 6

What if our Creator had spoken only one star into existence? No doubt that star would be wondrous, just like everything He has made. But He chose instead to create billions of them—each with its own special way of lighting up the night sky. The psalmist reminds us that God determines the number of stars and calls them by name. Just like people. The story unfolding around us is not just about us—it's about the neighbor, the stranger, the precious souls all over the earth that we may never even meet in this life. Like constellations, our lives are intertwined in mysterious patterns, woven together to tell a larger story. We are all called to shine His light in different ways, in different places. And we are infinitely more beautiful when we shine together.

He counts the number of the stars;
He gives names to all of them.
PSALM 147:4 HCSB

SEPTEMBER 7

Some days seem entirely impossible. Projects at work piled up like the dishes in our kitchen sink. No nap for the kids (or the mama). Bills that add up to more than what's in our bank account. Dust bunnies threatening to take over the floors. Toddler meltdowns at the store. It can be overwhelming.

But when we stand beside the Lord, nothing is impossible. He provides stamina and energy to get up with the baby in the dark of night. He offers peace when we are anything but peaceful. He gifts us with His presence when we need comfort. He promises to send joy in the morning. He is the same God who blessed Mary with an impossible pregnancy and sent salvation to the world in an impossibly small infant. He is a God of impossibilities. With Him, nothing is off limits. Take a breath—you've got this.

Nothing is impossible with God.
LUKE 1:37 NLT

SEPTEMBER 8

To begin with: a love so vast it can't be measured...a hope so sure it never disappoints... and grace so beautiful it's beyond our comprehension. We think about all we can praise God for—and we know a lifetime won't be enough. It doesn't have to be, because every blessing He gives is eternal, and we have all eternity to praise Him.

Think about all you can praise
God for and be glad about.
PHILIPPIANS 4:8 TLB

SEPTEMBER 9

Interrupted sleep, busy days, and loads of work have you feeling weary. Whether caring for a newborn baby, an active school-age student, or a temperamental teen, fatigue is weighing you down. Beyond tired, you fear sitting still for more than a few minutes because you know that you'll nod off if you close your eyes.

It's okay to be tired and it's okay to need to rest; Jesus asks you to come to Him. Resting is not giving up; no, resting is recharging. It's refueling. Resting in Jesus means that your burden is eased by His care and your heart is comforted by His love.

Come to Me, all of you who are weary and burdened, and I will give you rest.
MATTHEW 11:28 HCSB

SEPTEMBER 10

The Christians in the city of Corinth were having a problem. Some of them were eating meat that had been sacrificed to idols, and others were getting super offended by this. Two sides and lots of anger. If you've scrolled through Facebook or watched the news, you see these extreme, angry views on every single topic imaginable. How do we judge when to be offended? When to just take it in stride and let it be? The apostle Paul encouraged the Corinthians to change their focus. Don't look to the debate and decide which side is "right." Instead, make sure that in whatever you do you're giving glory to God. So, whether I eat or drink, or work or stay home, or breastfeed or bottle feed, or sleep train or co-sleep, or homeschool or public school or whatever I do, I want it all to be for the glory of God!

Therefore, whether you eat or drink, or whatever you do, do everything for God's glory.
I CORINTHIANS 10:31 HCSB

SEPTEMBER 11

You've spent so long hoping, waking up to fear raining down hard, and you just want to close your eyes and forget the daylight a little longer. Then hope digs in its heels and refuses to let go of God's promise to care for you and calm the storm. Whatever you're hoping for is in Him—and it's coming.

He calms the storm, so that its waves are still.
PSALM 107:29 NKJV

SEPTEMBER 12

You have the distinct privilege of experiencing all the feelings that come with watching your children grow up. You celebrate with them in the happy things, you hurt with them in the hard things, and you feel every other emotion with them in between. Sometimes these moments happen in the presence of others, but God has graciously reserved the most tender moments just for you. The time you sat on her bed and comforted her as she sorted through her feelings between sobs. The time he courageously told you about his dream for the future with all the details perfectly thought out. These vulnerable times can really surprise us, and the perfect words don't always come to us right away. It's these treasured times that we ponder in our hearts afterward, relying on the Holy Spirit to give us words to share with our children that point directly to Him.

But Mary treasured up all these things
and pondered them in her heart.
LUKE 2:19 NIV

SEPTEMBER 13

When we head for the gym, we probably don't expect it to be easy. We know building muscle requires exertion. We can't walk in, stand there, stare at people on their machines, and expect it to make any difference in our own bodies. Change requires some discomfort. Discomfort creates growth. And who doesn't want to grow in some way? The same thing happens in our spirits. We can't expect deep change to happen if our faith is a spectator sport. We may marvel at an awesome sermon, or highlight every page in the latest book, but unless we dig in and walk out what we're learning, it's no better than standing by watching the weight lifters. Let's ask the Lord where He might be calling us to take a step today that leads to a stronger, more vibrant faith tomorrow!

Be doers of the word, and not hearers only.
JAMES 1:22 ESV

SEPTEMBER 14

Life just comes at us some days, leaving us tired, faith-tested, and squinting to see hope in the middle of the mayhem. But we have a Father who comes to us, with comfort to quiet the questions and strength to stand up and keep going. And the hope we can't bear to see disappear? He's got that too. It comes alongside His promise, "I will never, never fail you nor forsake you" (Hebrews 13:5 TLB).

God will tenderly comfort you.... He will give you the strength to endure.

II CORINTHIANS 1:7 TLB

SEPTEMBER 15

How many times have you placed your Bible on the nightstand, intending to read a few chapters before bed? The first few evenings go well, and Scripture dances through your heart as you fall asleep. But then the kids aren't sleeping well, Netflix binges beckon, and reading is skipped so sleep can come earlier. Vows are made to pick the Bible back up the next night, but somehow it just doesn't happen.

If the Word is at the forefront of our day, our heart, our life, we'll be plugged into the Source from the start. And like the night-lights in our kids' rooms, it's only when we're plugged in that our light is able to shine. God promises that the Word gives life to all, that His life gives light that cannot be extinguished. Let's plug in.

In the beginning the Word already existed.
The Word was with God, and the Word was God.
JOHN 1:1 NLT

SEPTEMBER 16

Sometimes when life is going smoothly, we may worry that the other shoe is going to drop. If there's not chaos somewhere in our days, guilt can creep into our hearts. Guilt and worry are not two things we are called to feel. There is no guilt or shame in enjoying your days, in loving your life, in celebrating the little moments that may actually be or become the big ones.

Today, soak up this day with your family. Whether it's a day of big or little moments, of delights or disappointments, of highs or lows. Make an intentional decision to let your heart be light and your focus be higher. Jesus tells us not to worry about everyday life; let's take Him at His word.

That is why I tell you not to worry about everyday life—whether you have enough food and drink, or enough clothes to wear. Isn't life more than food, and your body more than clothing?

MATTHEW 6:25 NLT

SEPTEMBER 17

Let's go through today with great joy in our hearts. The joy that God's giving ignites in us. The kind that doesn't depend on circumstance but changes our outlook about what we're going through. Smile a lot. Laugh without holding back. Tell someone a happy story. Just be joyful—and enjoy seeing how His joy blesses others.

God had given us cause for great joy.
NEHEMIAH 12:43 TLB

SEPTEMBER 18

Do you ever find yourself rehashing an argument in your head that happened weeks ago? Do you blush remembering something you did years ago?

Sometimes our sins loom large in our own eyes. We feel bitterly sorry for them, have even repented, but we can't seem to shake the memory of them. We easily forget that grace has filled us up to overflowing, leaving no room for shame to shame us. Paul tells the church in Rome that there is no condemnation, no accusation from God, no judgment from Him, and no disapproval when we are in Christ Jesus.

When these shortcomings pop up in your head, turn and tell them to take flight! The Spirit has set you free in Christ Jesus from sin, death, and its shame!

There is therefore now no condemnation for those who are in Christ Jesus. For the law of the Spirit of life has set you free in Christ Jesus from the law of sin and death.

ROMANS 8:1–2 ESV

SEPTEMBER 19

Being tired is just a given when you enter the world of parenting. We have been expending our physical, mental, and emotional energy on our kids from the moment they took their first breath. It's not that feeding babies, changing diapers, and rocking them to sleep is actually hard to do. It's just so...constant. Yes, their needs change as they get older, but the demand of it all is just the same.

The nonstop nature of our job as mothers can regularly cause us to feel tired and weak, making even the simplest of tasks seem impossible. But hallelujah for a God we can call on at all times to give us His strength when we are depleted. Whether we are lacking sleep, lacking sense, or lacking self-control, all it takes is one sincerely uttered plea for help. He can be trusted to answer.

I can do all things through Christ
who strengthens me.
PHILIPPIANS 4:13 NKJV

SEPTEMBER 20

It's all good…because He's always good. When the worries pile up a little and our faith wears a little thin and our hearts need a little more hope for the day—it's all in Him. He'll take what's hindering our hearts and give what's healing and helpful. Love does that because it's all love can do—the good, the grace-filled, and the best.

Give all your worries and cares to God, for He cares about you.
I PETER 5:7 NLT

SEPTEMBER 21

That moment of takeoff on an airplane... somehow it never gets old. We gain a fresh perspective: trees and buildings that once towered over us are made into miniatures far below us; what was familiar becomes delightfully new. Life can be like that. We can get used to our little bubble and the people in it—home, church, school, neighborhood. We've taken that drive so many times, we forget what (or who!) we see along the way. Our world can shrink down and we can forget the countless possibilities, natural wonders, and simple blessings God provides at every turn.

When we find ourselves in a rut, let's change things up a bit. Walk instead of drive. Maybe introduce ourselves to someone we haven't met. Spend some time with a child to experience the world through their eyes. Let's ask God each day to help us see the ways He makes all things new.

Behold, I am making all things new.
REVELATION 21:5 ESV

SEPTEMBER 22

Chef. Chauffeur. Entertainer. Activities director. Housekeeper. Bankroller. Household organizer. Short-order cook. Caretaker. Tear wiper. Boo-boo kisser. Listener. Advisor. Breadwinner. Calendar keeper. Laundress. Shopper. Decorator.

While moms may need to fill each of these roles at some point, we are not made to be all things to all people all the time. We may be gifted in one or more of these areas, but no one person is fabulous at them all. When we try to be all things to all people in one day, things fall apart by noon. We cannot do it.

But there is One who can be—and is—all things. Jesus is a Wonderful Counselor, Mighty God, Everlasting Father, and Prince of Peace. Only Jesus, the One who came to make a mother and save the world, is all things. Only Him. Not us. This is truly good news.

For a Child is born to us, a Son is given to us.
The government will rest on His shoulders.
And He will be called: Wonderful Counselor,
Mighty God, Everlasting Father, Prince of Peace.
ISAIAH 9:6 NLT

SEPTEMBER 23

Today might not reveal the whys of what God is doing, but we can trust that in the waiting, our hearts are growing stronger. He's going to act on our behalf, and it's going to be absolute and amazing. What He makes happen isn't temporary or fleeting—it's blessing without sorrow and favor for a lifetime. So stay hopeful and wait for it, because it's going to be more than you imagined.

Rest in the Lord; wait patiently for Him to act.
PSALM 37:7 TLB

SEPTEMBER 24

The valley you're walking through is long and dark with no light in sight. Perhaps it is an illness or the illness of someone you love. Maybe it's a financial struggle or mental battle. Whatever it is, Jesus is near you. He promises to be there for you whenever you pray. The valley has a way of helping you draw nearer to Him than you ever have before. His presence fills not only your heart, but the universe. Call on His name, sweet friends; He's only a prayer away.

The Lord is near to all who call on Him,
to all who call on Him in truth.
PSALM 145:18 ESV

SEPTEMBER 25

Anxiety comes on us in an instant. That horrible pulse-pounding, headache-inducing anxiety can cripple us as we try to mother and lead our family.

The good news is that God is close at hand even in difficult times. He doesn't want us to be anxious about anything. Instead, He asks us to pray about everything.

He then promises to send His peace, peace that is so extreme we can't even understand it. But it gets better! This peace will guard our hearts and minds.

God's promises are not just "Oh, I'll see what I can do." He doesn't promise to only think about what we've asked. He commands us to make our requests known and He follows up with overwhelming, unimaginable peace and a guard on our hearts and minds.

Make your requests known to Him and watch Him follow through with strong peace!

The Lord is at hand; do not be anxious about anything, but in everything by prayer and supplication with thanksgiving let your requests be made known to God. And the peace of God, which surpasses all understanding, will guard your hearts and your minds in Christ Jesus.

PHILIPPIANS 4:5–7 ESV

SEPTEMBER 26

They won't stop chasing us down, God's amazing goodness and unfailing love. We want them to overtake us today. We want them to roll over our souls like a wild, unexpected wave. They're going to wash away discouragement and sadness and refresh our world-weary hearts. They're what we want, God…so bring them on with all Your powerful, perfect heart.

Surely Your goodness and unfailing love
will pursue me all the days of my life.
PSALM 23:6 NLT

SEPTEMBER 27

The classic childhood game of hide-and-seek never seems to lose its flair. Kids love the thrill of finding a good hiding place and being quiet and still so they won't be found. But when the hunt is on, the seeker has the most exciting job of all. When they find a friend, their squeals of surprise and delight are followed by a wild chase to safety.

In the Christian life, we are the seekers who are looking for God. The difference is, we can't hide from God, and God isn't hiding from us. He challenges us to look for Him wholeheartedly. He's waiting to be found. He wants to be found. He will be found. That's His promise.

If you look for Me wholeheartedly, you will find Me.
JEREMIAH 29:13 NLT

SEPTEMBER 28

Even the most organized mama has to deal with a little chaos now and then, because...KIDS! We may have great intentions for a regular prayer time, or at least a conversation with Jesus throughout the day... But some seasons of life make it tougher to stop and connect. So how about adding a few touchstones to our days? Little reminders of God's love in the midst of the busyness. No matter how clean or cluttered our surroundings are at the moment, what if we walk through our homes and add a touch of sacred to our spaces? Kitchen sink, mudroom, laundry, bathroom...place a simple, tangible reminder to those spots where we spend lots of time and energy. When we see them, they'll invite us to pause, take a breath, and turn our hearts toward Him.

Then Samuel took a stone and set it up between Mizpah and Shen. He named it Ebenezer, saying, "Thus far the LORD has helped us."
I SAMUEL 7:12 NIV

SEPTEMBER 29

You're going to be brave today. You're going to dig deep into the truth of what God says about you and not spend a moment believing otherwise. You aren't what other people say about you, you aren't condemned for making a mistake, and you don't have to spend a minute feeling guilty before you feel forgiven. Be strong and believe: you are priceless…you are loved…you are whole…you are the joy of God's heart.

Make me walk along the right paths, for I know how delightful they really are.
PSALM 119:35 TLB

SEPTEMBER 30

Your desire is to spend time with God each day, but sometimes it just doesn't happen. Children get sick, someone calls off work, or other circumstances get in the way. While it's tempting to give in, choosing time with God will grow your faith and enable you to deal with all the "extra" circumstances. You never know what God wants to do through your faithfulness to Him. The next time your quiet time is interrupted, grab a few spare minutes in the student pickup line, an office waiting room, or between errands. He only wants to speak to and listen to your heart.

Walk in obedience to Him, and keep His decrees and commands, His laws and regulations, as written in the Law of Moses.
I KINGS 2:3 NIV

OCTOBER 1

The end of summer can be exciting. With warm boots, cozy sweaters, and oversized hoodies, it's hard not to get a little eager for the fall season to begin. Putting on the new season's clothes can be a reminder of what God suggests we wear in every season too. No, not holy vestments. Instead, He says mercy and kindness are the latest craze.

Sometimes it doesn't come easy to extend mercy and kindness to our kids, husbands, and others around us. In those times, maybe it would help if we visualized what it might look like to figuratively grab mercy and kindness by the collar and step into it. What if we closed our eyes and let mercy and kindness become who and what we are? Who knows? Maybe this will lead us to love instead of judgment.

Since God chose you to be the holy people He loves, you must clothe yourselves with tenderhearted mercy, kindness, humility, gentleness, and patience.

COLOSSIANS 3:12 NLT

OCTOBER 2

Busy is the new fine. The standard answer to "How are you?" used to be "Fine." But today when people are asked how they are, the answer is usually "Busy!" which is followed by empathetic nods. We've moved from giving each other an emotional response with a smile to a physical response with a sigh. Our fast-paced world values activity and productivity—and so does God—but He also knows the value of rest. How can you follow His example and align your values with His? You could start by making time for your own version of "seventh day" rest to give yourself a true break from busy. Maybe you will take a nap, take a bath, or read that book that's been collecting dust on your nightstand. Whatever you do, resist the urge to be productive now, and you will be better prepared to tackle your to-do list later.

On the seventh day God had finished His work of creation, so He rested from all His work. And God blessed the seventh day and declared it holy, because it was the day when He rested from all His work of creation.

GENESIS 2:2–3 NLT

OCTOBER 3

Children put their complete trust in those who care for them. They have a joy in them that's so remarkable, so like the light of God's presence. How does growing up challenge our trust in our perfect Father and restrain our joy? Today, let's ask Him to renew our childlike trust and refresh the brightness of that contagious joy sent straight from His heart—and believe He'll be faithful to give it.

See how very much our Father loves us, for He calls us His children, and that is what we are!
I JOHN 3:1 NLT

OCTOBER 4

Newsflash: Our children are always listening to our lives. Not just what we say to them but the words we speak about them, about ourselves, about others. If we want them to believe they're everything God says they are, then let's speak His words over them. If we want them to grow up with a deep sense of the self-worth He's woven into them, then let's stop speaking negatively about ourselves. And if we want to plant seeds of kindness toward others in their hearts, let's allow those things to bloom in our own hearts first.

What are we saying about people? Are we celebrating the good, or pointing out the flaws? We're the first narrators of the life story unfolding around them. How are we choosing to tell it?

No foul language is to come from your mouth, but only what is good for building up someone in need, so that it gives grace to those who hear.
EPHESIANS 4:29 HCSB

OCTOBER 5

Before an airplane takes off, the crew makes safety announcements. They remind passengers to "place an oxygen mask on yourself before assisting others." While it goes against our own tendencies, people truly need their own oxygen before they can be of any good to someone else. As parents, there is nothing we wouldn't do for our kids—including depriving ourselves of that which is life-giving.

But God doesn't tell us to do this. God tells us to rest. When He created the world, God worked really hard, and then He rested. Rest is vital for our own well-being and to help us care for those around us. Even the Lord modeled this—and if He can make time, so can we. Carve out time for a walk, to take a nap, or to read a book—whatever gives your heart rest. Put your oxygen mask on and breathe.

By the seventh day God had finished the work He had been doing; so on the seventh day He rested from all His work. Then God blessed the seventh day and made it holy, because on it He rested from all the work of creating that He had done.

GENESIS 2:2–3 NIV

OCTOBER 6

Everything that happens in our lives is a direct effect of God's love, and its purpose is to put a floodlight on our need for Him. Some things humble, extracting fragments of pride we didn't realize were keeping parts of us from all of Him. It's always working good stuff in and bad stuff out, the refining love of God. It gives us an even clearer view of the cross and the One who carried it—the One who now carries us.

Through the death on the cross…Christ has brought you into the very presence of God, and you are standing there before Him with nothing left against you.
COLOSSIANS 1:22 TLB

OCTOBER 7

"But God, I just don't understand."

You try your best to wrap your mind around the circumstances, but no matter how hard you try, you just can't seem to understand what God is doing. You want to, but it doesn't make sense.

Life isn't fair. God is in the business of taking the worst circumstances and making them the best. His redemption plan is always for your good and His glory. Trust Him with everything you have and don't rely on your comprehension. The One who holds the heavens in place guards your heart in peace.

Trust in the LORD with all your heart and lean not on your own understanding.
PROVERBS 3:5 NIV

OCTOBER 8

Has your child ever mimicked you? Maybe told a joke you always tell? Or even the words you use when you're upset?

God set up families so there would be a place for children to mimic, follow, and learn from their parents. Children are supposed to copy their parents. Sometimes that responsibility is weighty. There are many things in our own lives we don't want our children to copy. We recognize those little eyes on us and wish they weren't always so perceptive. Instead, let's use those constant eyes on us to inspire us to keep our own eyes on Jesus. As we look to our Savior and joyfully strive to follow Him in every area of our lives, we'll be able to say to our children, "Watch me! Follow me! I'm following Jesus's example so you can follow mine!"

Follow my example, as I follow the example of Christ.
1 CORINTHIANS 11:1 NIV

OCTOBER 9

Your calendar is full of things you have to do, things you need to do, and things you want to do. Whatever you are doing every day—whether you've formally scheduled time for it or not—you've said yes to it. Your yeses are an investment of your time and energy and will always produce some sort of return. Short-term investments rely on your own abilities to produce quick, temporary returns. Long-term investments require persistence, patience, perseverance, and reliance on God to produce lasting returns. These are the investments that cause us to become weary of waiting, question our decisions, and make us want to throw in the towel—if we look through a short-term lens. Isn't that the perfect picture of the mothering marathon? Don't give up on the time and energy you are investing in your children. The Lord promises a harvest of blessing at just the right time!

So let's not get tired of doing what is good.
At just the right time, we will reap a
harvest of blessing if we don't give up.
GALATIANS 6:9 NLT

OCTOBER 10

We like to take part in our battles. They keep us up at night and stand ready to face us in the morning. But in every moment of every battle, we're protected by the One who is on the front line day and night—fighting for our win without a closed eye or a turned shoulder. God is at our defense and He doesn't fail—and the end will always find us in His favor.

Don't be discouraged…for the battle is not yours, but God's.
II CHRONICLES 20:15 NLT

OCTOBER 11

We mamas think of our children countless times a day. Whether they're playing in the next room or living across the world, they're never far from our hearts. Because they're so precious to us, we may struggle with worry about them—their choices, their health, their safety... The list goes on. But good news! God desires to transform those fears into faith. And when that happens, we experience more joy (Proverbs 12:25); we live with more peace (Philippians 4:6); and we have a greater sense of confidence and assurance (Psalm 55:22). While we all know squelching worry altogether is no small task, little steps in the right direction will make a huge difference in the long run. We can start by digging into His Word regarding specific fears we face. Let's keep those promises in our hearts and speak them every time our children come to mind.

When I am afraid, I will trust in You.
PSALM 56:3 HCSB

OCTOBER 12

There's a scene in the movie *Moana* that brings on the ugly cry. It's toward the end, when Moana realizes that without her heart, the beautiful Te Fiti has become a fiery lava monster. Moana gently reminds her of who she is, saying, "I have crossed the horizon to find you, I know your name..." She replaces Te Fiti's heart, and everything that was dead comes back to life.

We know the One who has crossed the eternal horizon...and returned to tell about it. He calls you by name. He says who you are, even when you have forgotten. No matter what, you are loved. And being loved is not being abandoned. Being loved is being welcomed. Being loved is intentional. Being loved is who you are—no matter what.

Now this is what the Lord says—
the One who created you, Jacob,
and the One who formed you, Israel—
"Do not fear, for I have redeemed you;
I have called you by your name; you are Mine."
ISAIAH 43:1 HCSB

OCTOBER 13

God moves things into place and brings people into our lives for His purposes. His love is for every heart. He wants the lost to be found, and we're the light that helps them see His love more clearly. The smallest act of kindness led by the greatest love of all can make all the difference in a life.

You are a guide…a light for people
who are lost in darkness.
ROMANS 2:19 NLT

OCTOBER 14

You saw the look in her eye as she passed you in the grocery aisle. Cultural differences and language barriers are part of her everyday normal as she attempts to make the adjustment to a new way of life in a new country. She picks up the can of carrots, and you can tell she wants to understand the label but doesn't. God loves to see your heart for her need. When you are embracing His compassionate ways, He bridges the gap through your smile and kind words. Whether a grocery store incident or some other situation, your hands and feet are serving as His. His comfort covers both the giver and the receiver!

The LORD comforts His people and will have compassion on His afflicted ones.
ISAIAH 49:13 NIV

OCTOBER 15

The book of Psalms is a beautiful example of how to pray to God. There are psalms crying out to God for help, psalms that reiterate promises made to God, and lots of praises to Him.

In Psalm 148 the psalmist instructs everything from the stars to the angels to the oceans and the cattle to praise the Lord. Why? How weird is it to tell the sun and moon to praise the Lord?

It's not weird when the Lord is our God. God is above all—greater than the splendor of a shooting star or the majesty of a mighty ocean. He is stronger than the mountains and brighter than light-ning. Yes, He does so much for us but more than anything He is worthy of our praise. His person, His being, His Name are to be exalted.

Join all of creation in praising Him today!

Praise the Lord. Praise the Lord from the heavens; praise Him in the heights above. Praise Him, all His angels; praise Him, all His heavenly hosts. Praise Him, sun and moon; praise Him, all you shining stars. Praise Him, you highest heavens and you waters above the skies.

PSALM 148:1–4 NIV

OCTOBER 16

Today might bring more than we can handle, but God didn't design us to go it alone here. He's got the help we need and He'll be the strength we need. We'll draw hope from His grace and trust and listen. He's going to tell our hearts what to do… and He'll direct our steps in perfect order.

I am with you always, even to the end of the world.
MATTHEW 28:20 TLB

OCTOBER 17

When was the last time you bragged about something you weren't good at? Probably never. No one likes to admit where they are weak, let alone brag about it. The truth is, most people try really hard to keep their shortcomings concealed. But those vulnerable places are where God works best, and mothering is full of those kinds of moments. We tend to beat ourselves up about our mistakes and inabilities, but what if we did a fist pump instead? Let's embrace the perspective of the apostle Paul and courageously cry out in our weakness, "YES, God! This is Your moment!" Imagine the glory we could deflect off of ourselves and place onto God when we allow His power to work through us to redeem all we are incapable of ourselves.

Each time he said, "My grace is all you need. My power works best in weakness." So now I am glad to boast about my weaknesses, so that the power of Christ can work through me.
II CORINTHIANS 12:9 NLT

OCTOBER 18

Ever find yourself wondering, Why is the news so discouraging? Why can't they focus on the good things for once? Of course we don't want to turn a blind eye to the hurt of the world around us, but we all need a reason to lighten up now and then! No matter what's trending online, we know the tide of good and evil will always ebb and flow in this life. Ecclesiastes 1:9 reminds us: "History merely repeats itself. It has all been done before. Nothing under the sun is truly new" (NLT). But then comes Jesus. And Good News takes on a whole new meaning.

We don't have to wait for a happy report to fill our hearts with hope today. The Light of the world has come, and He's not going anywhere without us. What the enemy intends for evil, God will always use for good. The battle may continue, but in Him, the victory's won.

The light shines in the darkness, and
the darkness has not overcome it.
JOHN 1:5 NIV

OCTOBER 19

You're strong in the Lord. You're the loved, valued, wonderfully created recipient of every blessing God gives. Nothing in this challenging, changing, uphill life can knock you far enough down to keep Him from lifting you up again. If fear comes, foil it with prayer. If stress presses in, breathe deep His peace. There's a courageous response to every curveball life throws—and every one of them is found in Him.

Be strong and of good courage, do not…be afraid…for the LORD your God, He is the One who goes with you. He will not leave you.

DEUTERONOMY 31:6 NKJV

OCTOBER 20

Kids are great at praying. To them, praying is just another conversation in their day (that they happen to be having with God). Over the years those prayers become deeper and more complex, changing as they grow up.

The ways we pray change, but the One to whom our prayers rise remains the same. God is the same God who walked in Eden, who flooded the earth and saved Noah, who sent His Son to be born in a manger and later took that Son home, who blinded Saul and turned his heart to Paul, and who meets us today on our own roads to Damascus.

No matter where you walk today, let God hear you. Whisper a prayer, or if you simply cannot, know that God understands what's in the silence. God hears your prayers.

Meanwhile, the moment we get tired in the waiting, God's Spirit is right alongside helping us along. If we don't know how or what to pray, it doesn't matter. He does our praying in and for us, making prayer out of our wordless sighs, our aching groans.

ROMANS 8:26 THE MESSAGE

OCTOBER 21

"How are you?" A sweet text from an old friend pops up on your phone and you smile. What a blessing to have friends who care! True friendship is a treasure, but sometimes people, "friends," will let you down. Choosing friends who are faithful can be a difficult task, but being a good friend doesn't have to be as tough. You've probably heard it said: "Be the kind of friend you want to have." What if you took a moment to send a "how are you?" text to an old friend right now? Be blessed!

One who has unreliable friends soon comes to ruin,
but there is a friend who sticks closer than a brother.
PROVERBS 18:24 NIV

OCTOBER 22

Let's not spend our moments worrying today. We have to give everything to God for anything to go right. The beauty of it is, He wants the exchange—our worries for His peace. And that's the thing about God and grace—our hearts always win because He loves us so much.

Will all your worries add a single moment to your life?
MATTHEW 6:27 TLB

OCTOBER 23

King Saul was chasing David. While David was running and hiding, scared and worried, God was working. And soon, God rescued him.

After his rescue David wrote a beautiful psalm proclaiming God a rock, a fortress, a savior, protector, a place of safety and shield. He sang about God training him for battle, making him nimble, leading him to safety, and giving him strength. He even recorded this: "You light a lamp for me. The Lord, my God, lights up my darkness."

Wow! Don't you want some of that? Are there parenting days you just need some light? In fact, you need someone to even light the lamp for you? Parenting can wear us down, make us feel defeated, unskilled, and without strength.

When you get to that dark place, ask God to light it up. Read Psalm 18 to encourage and remind you of our strengthening, light-bringing God!

You light a lamp for me. The Lord, my God, lights up my darkness.
PSALM 18:28 NLT

OCTOBER 24

Every once in a while, the deep love we have for our children rises to the surface and surprises us. Our feelings can be so intense that they actually overwhelm us and bring us to tears. We look at our children in utter amazement, giving thanks to God for the blessing of being their mother. We love them with as much love as a person can possibly contain. Our motherly love is so real and so raw that we can't even describe it. All we can do is feel it and acknowledge the presence of the inexpressible love flowing through every single part of our being. This must be the way the Lord loves His children, and how He wants us to love Him in return. Are we living our lives with an ever-flowing, overflowing love for the Lord?

You must love the Lord your God with all your heart, all your soul, all your mind, and all your strength.

MARK 12:30 NLT

OCTOBER 25

There are gifts in giving God control. Peace comes...joy returns...hope emerges...and our hearts can rest. It's natural to want control, unnerving to let go—unless we put all into God's hands. He's so careful with us. He understands us, how we're wired, how hard it is for us to just trust. And so there's grace, reminding us of the sacrifice that made us whole, and we know that surrendering all is always best.

I made you and I will care for you.
ISAIAH 46:4 TLB

OCTOBER 26

Good things come to those who ______. How would you finish this sentence? To those who wait? Those who pray? Those who try really hard not to mess up? There are so many unknowns in life—wouldn't it be nice just once to have a simple equation that guarantees all will be well?

People often tried pinning Jesus down to give them answers. They wanted life to run smoothly, and they figured He was the man for the job. But His response was rarely as straightforward as they'd hoped. They wanted black and white, and He gave them gray. They wanted buttoned-up solutions, and He told them stories. He knew the assurance they were seeking would never be found in a formula; it would be found in Him. It's good for us to remember that too.

For all the promises of God find their Yes in him.
II CORINTHIANS 1:20 ESV

OCTOBER 27

There is a myth that many moms have bought into, hook, line, and sinker. We've managed to convince ourselves that balance is something we can obtain and sustain, and that's just not true.

The laundry will always pile up. Same with the dishes, the guilt, and the "in-a-minutes." We will never be caught up, because nothing good is ever finished. There is and will always be more to clean, more to schedule, more to shop for, more to wrap up, more ideas and goals and problems. BUT we can rest in the midst of the undone, and we can welcome God's grace. While balance may be a myth, grace is very real and available in spades. Every night offers the chance to lay your head down with a smile because you gave it a go, and God was there, and He'll be there tomorrow too.

"My grace is all you need. My power works best in weakness." So now I am glad to boast about my weaknesses, so that the power of Christ can work through me. That's why I take pleasure in my weaknesses, and in the insults, hardships, persecutions, and troubles that I suffer for Christ. For when I am weak, then I am strong.

II CORINTHIANS 12:9–10 NLT

OCTOBER 28

Every kind thing we do makes some kind of difference. Our lives are busy and weighed down with all the things we think need to be done, when really all we need to do is love each other and be kind. God's got the rest. He's got our provision, our strength, and the plans that truly matter. So let's just trust Him so we can get busy being kind.

Be kind to each other, tenderhearted, forgiving one another, just as God through Christ has forgiven you.
EPHESIANS 4:32 NLT

OCTOBER 29

Do you love listening to the voice of your child? Every mother does. Hearing your baby's cry for the first time is unforgettable. But as your baby grows, hearing her say "Mama" (or Daddy) for the first time is even more unforgettable.

If you love your baby this much, imagine how much your Maker loves to hear your voice. And when you lift your voice in praise? He is lifted and adored; oh, how He loves to hear your praises. Perhaps you could remind Him of your love and devotion in this moment?

I will praise the Lord all my life; I will sing praise to my God as long as I live.
PSALM 146:2 NIV

OCTOBER 30

Are you one of those people that keep your baby's name a secret before they are born? Do you choose unique names for your kids or classics?

God has exalted His Son's name above every name. The name of Jesus will one day bring every creature to its knees and cause every tongue to shout, "Jesus is Lord!"

There are days in parenting when everything seems to be against you (your kids especially!) and nothing you do, nothing you say seems to turn your day aright. When your day is stuck and your prayers are too, simply call on the name of Jesus. Whisper His name as a prayer. Or shout it in praise and adoration. Call on the name of Jesus!

If everything under heaven must bow, even your day can be turned with the power of His name. Keep His name on your lips!

Therefore God has highly exalted him and bestowed on him the name that is above every name, so that at the name of Jesus every knee should bow, in heaven and on earth and under the earth, and every tongue confess that Jesus Christ is Lord, to the glory of God the Father.

PHILIPPIANS 2:9–11 ESV

OCTOBER 31

The vibrant, life-giving, breathtaking beauty of our Lord is always with us—ready to bring light…to give life…to draw others to Him. It's a powerful privilege, carrying His indescribable love within us—and our most important purpose is to let it shine.

Let your light shine for all to see. For the glory of the L*ORD* *rises to shine on you.*
ISAIAH 60:1 NLT

NOVEMBER 1

Feeling fear is part of being a human, and it's not a bad thing! Fear is a God-given emotion that serves an important purpose in our lives. At its essence, the purpose of fear is to keep us safe. It warns us of danger and helps us make decisions that keep us from harm. Experiencing some fear is normal, but when we are overcome with it, it's time to call on the Lord. It's no different than when our children are afraid and come to us for help. We take them in our arms, wipe away their tears, and comfort them with our words...but our presence is really all they need. That's exactly what our Father does for us if we draw near to Him when we are afraid. He reminds us who He is, tells us how strong He is, and promises to help us. Thank You, Lord!

Do not fear, for I am with you; do not be afraid, for I am your God. I will strengthen you; I will help you; I will hold on to you with My righteous right hand.
ISAIAH 41:10 HCSB

NOVEMBER 2

Walking through a playroom in the middle of the night can be downright dangerous. Do those tiny toys multiply in the darkness and plan strategies to destroy our bare feet? How many times have we told our kids, "If you'd just put it away right after playing with it..." But they forget. Things pile up, and then we're faced with a middle-of-the-night obstacle course.

It's a perfect picture of what sin can do in our lives. Often it starts small—little things left unchecked here and there. We get sloppy; we compromise; we justify. And suddenly the enemy has taken all our broken pieces and planned a strategic effort to bring us down. What's the answer? Turn on the light! See that soul clutter for what it is. Call on Jesus to help us clear the way again. Stop allowing negative thoughts, attitudes, and actions to pile up, and live a little freer every day.

Again Jesus spoke to them, saying, "I am the light of the world. Whoever follows me will not walk in darkness, but will have the light of life."

JOHN 8:12 ESV

NOVEMBER 3

We live to be poured out for God—to allow Him to create in us a pure heart, to be used for His purposes. He gave each of us special gifts for our journey, and He'll ignite them with passion. What we love to do—what sets our hearts aflame and gets us excited to be alive—is the given gift God will use for His glory.

Through Christ, all the kindness of God
has been poured out upon us.
ROMANS 1:5 TLB

NOVEMBER 4

Women constantly perform tiny acts of service. The bittiest of details, done with barely a thought. Women are the keepers of the minutiae, of the details that make a home run and hearts sing. We are the knowers of small things, of favorite items and things not-so-loved. We can read a heart in one glance. We can heal with a hug. We can calm with a word. We are the hosts of each other, the middle-of-the-night texters, the hearts that reach out when we feel a friend needs us. Women are the unseen do-ers. We are the people of hidden service, who have learned to do things swiftly and silently in a second-nature sort of way.

Each and every one of those invisible tasks is seen, etched in God's mind as He delights in you. You are beloved to Him. God delights in His daughters (that's you!)

The Lord your God is living among you.
He is a mighty savior.
He will take delight in you with gladness.
With His love, He will calm all your fears.
He will rejoice over you with joyful songs.
ZEPHANIAH 3:17 NLT

NOVEMBER 5

How many times have you prayed for something to turn out right and then it does? Maybe something small like a thunderstorm not waking your baby? Or something more serious like direction in a hard situation?

When the baby slept through the storm and you made the right choice, did you immediately thank God for coming through? Or did you just say, "Whew. That was a close one?"

Purpose in your heart to make note of when God answers your prayer. Maybe jot it down in a journal, mark your calendar with a star, or simply stop and say a heartfelt "thank You."

This isn't to make sure God will come through again (He doesn't keep score), it's to turn your heart to His goodness and remind yourself that God will always come through!

But God did listen! He paid attention to my prayer.
PSALM 66:19 NLT

NOVEMBER 6

God is aware of every breath and every moment. He won't step away from being our way through any storm. It rages; we rest—in His love, faithfulness, and assurance that He's got this. He'll still the winds and calm the waters, and our hearts will come out of it stronger than ever.

God never abandons us. We get knocked down, but we get up again and keep going.
II CORINTHIANS 4:9 TLB

NOVEMBER 7

A mother's heart is full of her best hopes and biggest dreams for her kids. She hopes they will be happy and full of joy. She hopes they will have a BFF who really gets them. She hopes they will have good health always. She hopes they will study hard and graduate. She hopes they will fall in love and build a beautiful family. She hopes they will find a good job doing something they enjoy. She hopes they will have a strong faith and share it with others. She never stops hoping and dreaming for the very best life for her kids. But at the same time, she is wise. She knows her hopes and dreams can't begin to compare to the good plans God has for their lives. She trusts Him completely with their future, because she knows His plan is perfect and full of hope.

"For I know the plans I have for you," says the Lord. *"They are plans for good and not for disaster, to give you a future and a hope."*
JEREMIAH 29:11 NLT

NOVEMBER 8

When we're caught up in the rush of the world, it can be hard to see beneath the surface of things. That takes time and energy, and who isn't stretched thin already? For instance, our children do things every day that make us go "Hmm…" or "Ugh!" or "Where-did-that-come-from?!"

We see what they do, hear what they say, and react accordingly. We give them consequences, move on, and pray they won't do it again (at least not before dinner!).

But God's Word reminds us that He's not about changing our behavior; He's about revealing the truth in our "innermost being" (Psalm 51:6). He knows what flows out of us comes from deep within us. And while few of us are able to sit down with our kids daily for long, soul-searching conversations, it can make a big difference to take a few moments to understand what's going on inside.

The spirit of a man is the lamp of the Lord,
searching all the inner depths of his heart.
PROVERBS 20:27 NKJV

NOVEMBER 9

Fear can grip us some days, casting a shadow over the light of God's love, the love we know is true and powerful and present. God never leaves us, even when worries find their way in, leaving our hearts fearful. Let's be brave and let God's perfect love extinguish it. There's no room for it today, here in the hand that holds the universe, the hand that's holding us. There's only peace and perfect love.

All the powers of hell itself cannot keep God's love away. Our fears for today, our worries about tomorrow.

ROMANS 8:38 TLB

NOVEMBER 10

Every woman has characteristics and traits she'd like to work on, improve, or even overcome. But since the good Lord made us by His design, hand-picking each and every bitty detail of who we are, isn't that how we should deal with all of ourselves? This isn't about nature vs. nurture. This is about shedding the guilt for that which makes us who we are, because who we are is His.

God hasn't given us a spirit of fear or self-deprecation; rather, He's instilled gratitude in our hearts. Let's practice appreciation instead of guilt and stop apologizing for who we are. Because we're His, and there's nothing to apologize for about that.

God has not given us a spirit of fear and timidity, but of power, love, and self-discipline.
II TIMOTHY 1:7 NLT

NOVEMBER 11

God loves you. On your hardest day as a mom, He loves you. God is with you. When you are alone, lonely, and juggling everything by yourself, He is with you. God is ready. The day you feel out of your element and out of ideas, God is ready to fulfill your needs. Today may "the God of our Lord Jesus Christ, the Father of glory...give you the Spirt of wisdom and of revelation in the knowledge of Him, having the eyes of your hearts enlightened, that you may know what is the hope to which He has called you."

He has chosen you for your children. He has you in the palm of His hand and no one can snatch you out. You are His beloved, the apple of His eye. Receive the blessing from His Word and walk in His hope as you mother your children today.

The God of our Lord Jesus Christ, the Father of glory, may give you the Spirit of wisdom and of revelation in the knowledge of Him, having the eyes of your hearts enlightened, that you may know what is the hope to which He has called you.

EPHESIANS 1:17–18 ESV

NOVEMBER 12

Being still keeps God moving in our lives. We trust He's doing what's best and putting our worries to rest. He loves us far too fully and faithfully to take us in any direction that isn't part of His plan for our lives—and it's all good.

Be still, and know that I am God.
PSALM 46:10 NKJV

NOVEMBER 13

The selfie phenomenon happening in our culture is an outward expression of an inward attitude. We are a culture obsessed with ourselves, and our social media feeds make that glaringly obvious. Selfies do all the talking: Look at me! Look at me with my friends! Look at me on vacation! Look at me at a concert! Look at me drinking coffee! Look at me and my cat! Look at me reading my Bible. (Ouch. That one hurt.) In this self-ie-paced world we're living in, it's a constant battle for parents and kids alike to keep the focus off of themselves. It won't be easy, but it can absolutely be done if we decide to take a stand for Him. How can we rearrange our priorities and establish a household that chooses to serve the Lord over serving ourselves?

But as for me and my family, we will serve the LORD.
JOSHUA 24:15 NLT

NOVEMBER 14

We may not realize everything we're signing up for when we have children—even those of us who read all the books, review all the blogs, sign up for all the classes. If we're control freaks by nature, we're in for huge changes, because one of the biggest lessons kids teach us is all about letting go. From the moment they join our families, we're forced to loosen our white-knuckled grasp on everything. We let go of tiny hands as they take first steps; we let go of our ability to shelter them as they venture into the world; we let go of expectations for their lives as we allow God to grow them in His way. (And we have the privilege of participating in that sometimes-glorious, sometimes-messy transformation!) We'll always hug them tight and hold them close in our hearts, but our greatest joy will be found in letting them fly.

I will teach all your children, and
they will enjoy great peace.
ISAIAH 54:13 NLT

NOVEMBER 15

They had reached the bottom of the barrel. All that was left in the cupboard were spices, and the fridge contained a half-empty jar of pickles. And so they prayed. "We believe You, Lord. We will eat dinner tonight!" And they went about their day with trust in their hearts.

He went off to work at the church, and she began working in the garden. Hours later as she walked around to the front of the house, she noticed bags on the front stoop. Someone had delivered a week's worth of groceries.

The Lord always delivers on His promises. We don't always know when or how, but we can believe. His eye is always on His beloved children.

For this reason I say to you, do not be worried about your life, as to what you will eat or what you will drink; nor for your body, as to what you will put on. Is not life more than food, and the body more than clothing?

MATTHEW 6:25 NASB

NOVEMBER 16

There used to be a show called Extreme Makeover: Home Edition. A family would be featured who had both endured trials and had a felt need for their home to be different. The family would leave on a vacation, and construction on their new home would happen around the clock for a week. The homeowners would weep through the reveal of their now beautiful and functional home, finally able to live in a space that worked for their family's needs.

What if there was a show titled Extreme Makeover: Heart Edition? We all have a need, a hope for an extreme makeover of our hearts. We don't need a camera crew or disastrous living conditions to qualify. We only need to ask the One who holds the master blueprints to do His best design work in our hearts, that others will see it and trust Him with their hearts too.

He put a new song in my mouth, a hymn of praise to our God. Many will see and fear and put their trust in the Lord.

PSALM 40:3 HCSB

NOVEMBER 17

It can be tempting to say you're "just a mom," unable to do big things for the Lord or for each other. But Jesus showed us that laying down our lives can be as simple as showing up. Jesus showed up among the sick, the prostitutes, and the shunned. He invited children to come to Him. Even while dying on the cross—the ultimate laying down of His life—Jesus was present, asking forgiveness on our behalf.

We can lay down our lives. Babysitting for a friend, picking up the phone to call a family member, visiting a neighbor… This kind of presence offered is an inconvenience, an interruption, and a blessing to both sides because it adds up to love. "Laying down our lives" always ends up in selfless, sacrificial love. We can show up for our families and friends, and therefore show them what love is.

This is how we know what love is: Jesus Christ laid down His life for us. And we ought to lay down our lives for our brothers and sisters.
I JOHN 3:16 NIV

NOVEMBER 18

At the root of every good thing is God's love. It's more vast than the universe and deeper than any ocean—and it's as good as it is fathomless. His love for us isn't moved by emotion; it's secured by grace. And it's rock solid. Nothing you've done and not a thing you do can keep Him from raining down on you with His remarkable, unrelenting love.

Three things will last forever—faith, hope, and love—and the greatest of these is love.
I CORINTHIANS 13:13 NLT

NOVEMBER 19

Encouraging one another doesn't sound so hard. A fist bump here, an "atta girl" there. A quick text to say, "You can do this!" Encouraging one another sounds pretty easy...until you realize it's not. If your emotions get in the way, it can actually be difficult to "encourage one another and build each other up." But the Lord doesn't give us a free pass to withhold encouragement because of jealousy or fear. Anytime we put our hearts on the line, we take a leap of faith. And in the leaping, we allow the Lord to hold our hand.

Offer the encouraging word nearly spilling from your lips. Grab the hand of God and let Him guide you. Following His lead will never let you down. Encourage one another and build each other up. Simple—and sometimes difficult—as that.

Therefore encourage one another and build each other up.
I THESSALONIANS 5:11 HCSB

NOVEMBER 20

Our plans for the day are subject to change, always, by the One whose counsel stands first and forever. If we surrender our moments to God, God will guide our steps, and our hearts will be able to take each one with grace—and trust where they lead with joy.

The counsel of the LORD stands forever, the plans of His heart to all generations.
PSALM 33:11 NKJV

NOVEMBER 21

Painting furniture is quite the process. The desk or dresser has to first be sandpapered smooth, which often takes longer than the actual painting. The scratches and imperfections and discolorations need to be sanded down so that the paint will adhere smoothly, resulting in a beautiful finish.

Motherhood provides tiny humans who will scrape against us like sandpaper, and (much like sanding furniture) softening comes more easily when we give in to the grit. Hardness happens when we fight against that which is intended to make us soft.

Mothering gives our hearts a chance to soften. In seasons of mothering tiny kids, they come first. And when we give in to the rhythms of our family instead of fighting them, we all become more beautiful.

He has made everything beautiful in its time. He has also set eternity in the human heart; yet no one can fathom what God has done from beginning to end.
ECCLESIASTES 3:11 NIV

NOVEMBER 22

Our path might be washed away by the pelting storms of things not happening as soon as we hoped and losing relationships we felt we needed most, but what we need most, what matters most of all, is the Lord getting close to our broken hearts and saying, "I am the One that even the wind and the waves obey." His words are light that covers our path with hope and love that never fails.

Your word is a lamp to my feet
and a light to my path.
PSALM 119:105 NKJV

NOVEMBER 23

Mothering may not look like what we thought it would look like. It actually looks like...sharing our food. It's grocery shopping—again. It's applying sunscreen to every inch of our kids' exposed skin, then forgetting to apply it to ourselves. It's walking slowly next to a toddler who "can do it herself!" It's coaching a middle schooler through feeling ALL THE FEELINGS in a day. Mothering is quietly completing the tasks no one will see but everyone would miss if left undone. It's making choices that are hard but right for your kids. It's letting your kids go. It's holding your kids close. Mothering is offering a prayer when you have no words to utter.

Mothering is delightful, difficult, beautiful, brutal, blessed, terrifying, sweet, good, and hard. Mothering is everything.

For everything there is a season,
a time for every activity under heaven.
ECCLESIASTES 3:1 NLT

NOVEMBER 24

God has you on a unique path. The gifts He's put in you will be engaged, the traits you have will be shaped for His glory, and there will be people along the way who need the love in your heart in a way only you can give it. They'll see the likeness of your Father in you, and that's the most beautiful part of the plan.

The Lord directs the steps of the godly.
PSALM 37:23 NLT

NOVEMBER 25

Our identity can get all wrapped up with our mothering. Our own hearts can get lost in the shuffle of the daily tasks, and in the bigger picture of all that we do. It's on those days that it's especially important to recall that before you were a mother, you were a woman. Before you were a wife, mother, student, employee, empty nester, or anything else—God first made you a woman. You were created for beauty right from His beauty. You are lovely, sweet, and funny. You radiate because of His love in your heart. And moms? You can do this. No matter how many kids you have, or how old they are… It's hard to mother, and it's sometimes hard to remember ourselves amid the mothering. Good thing God never forgets exactly who He made us to be—beautiful humans, created in His image.

So God created human beings in His own image. In the image of God He created them; male and female He created them. Then God blessed them and said, "Be fruitful and multiply. Fill the earth and govern it. Reign over the fish in the sea, the birds in the sky, and all the animals that scurry along the ground."

GENESIS 1:27–28 NLT

NOVEMBER 26

God never leaves you, and He never loses sight of what He created you to do. You are in His thoughts, engraved on His hand, and surrounded by His love. What matters to you matters to Him, and there's no one on earth who can take your place. His purposes for you will come to pass, with perfect love, at the perfect time.

I have formed you, you are My servant...
you will not be forgotten by Me!
ISAIAH 44:21 NKJV

NOVEMBER 27

Hold a tiny acorn. Turn it over in your hand. Look for evidence of…anything? It looks so harmless. Squirrel food, you think.

Now look up at the oak tree the acorn fell from. Seventy feet tall, shaking with strength in the wind. It houses the squirrels who eat its food. It shelters animals and people. Its wood can be used to make some of the strongest furniture you can buy. But where did it come from?

That incredible power, or the potential for it, lives inside one tiny acorn. It doesn't take two or three acorns, just one.

The Holy Spirit lives in you. It doesn't take more than one person, just you. To do the impossible. To serve with power. To stand strong in the midst of storms.

You are from God, little children, and have overcome them; because greater is He who is in you than he who is in the world.
I JOHN 4:4 NASB

NOVEMBER 28

Our relationships. A new house. Becoming financially stable. There are so many things we can put our hope in. It's so tempting to think that whenever that situation is smoothed out, or that promise is fulfilled, or that event has passed… only then, at that time, will everything be okay. But the reality is that having hope in anything besides Jesus holds the chance of letting us down. We may become disenchanted with the relationship. The furnace may need to be replaced. The paycheck may not stretch far enough. And the things of this world will rust, tarnish, and fade.

When we put all of our eggs in the basket of the world, one by one they will break. But the love of our Lord? That is forever strong, never disappointing, always present, and eternally faithful. We can place our hope, trust, and love in Him without disappointment.

Trust steadily in God, hope unswervingly, love extravagantly. And the best of the three is love.
I CORINTHIANS 13:13 THE MESSAGE

NOVEMBER 29

The project deadline has just been cut from four months to one week. And if you don't complete it on time, the entire company will miss its deadline and lose thousands of potential dollars. Can you do it?

Because you believe in the power of partnership with Jesus, you say yes. And a miracle unfolds. People chip in. The project gets done. The customer is happy. But more importantly, you've seen God at work in a way you will never forget.

Pay close attention to the impossible opportunities that cross your path. They may be the perfect time to say no. And they may be just the way God wants to show up and amaze you.

Nothing will be impossible with God.
LUKE 1:37 NASB

NOVEMBER 30

What's done is done. The past is past. If it was good, revel in the completion of it. If it was bad, be thankful that the blood of Jesus covers all. But there's just way too much now to spend time worrying about then. Focus on what is going on around you and how you fit into it all. There's so much opportunity within your current reach, and you don't want to miss it!

The beautiful thing is, the more you dwell in the present with the Lord, the more it sets you up for the future He has planned for you. So the only tense you need to focus on today is the present.

Jesus said to him, "No one, after putting his hand to the plow and looking back, is fit for the kingdom of God."
LUKE 9:62 NASB

DECEMBER 1

Kids dream of growing up to be astronauts, firefighters, and teachers. They dream of becoming president, scientists, and gourmet chefs. Kids are amazing at dreaming big, of having high hopes, and of believing they just may come true. When was the last time we, as moms, had big hopes and dreams? Right there in the middle of a crumb-covered kitchen or an empty nest, we can hope for big impossible things. Because when we trust in God, there is hope for the really big dreams, the huge goals, and the seemingly unattainable happy endings. All that which we don't currently have, we can hope for because "hope that is seen is no hope at all."

For in this hope we were saved. But hope that is seen is no hope at all. Who hopes for what they already have?
ROMANS 8:24 NIV

DECEMBER 2

Live today fully and joyfully. Live like you're filled with the life-changing love of God—because you are. Let His more-than-your-heart-can-hold love overflow into actions motivated by compassion and words saturated with kindness and hope. Let love radiate from you in smiles that light up lives and hugs that give comfort. All love, all day…and all for God's glory.

Your unfailing love will last forever. Your faithfulness is as enduring as the heavens.
PSALM 89:2 NLT

DECEMBER 3

Husband gets a speeding ticket. *Thank You, Lord, for reminding us to stay safe.* Coffee shop is out of that one drink you count on every day. *Thank You for reminding me what I can live without.* Daughter gets her first C and comes home in tears. *Thank You for challenging us to work through difficult circumstances.*

Everything we face has kingdom value. It can all be cashed in for treasure. And it's often the things that seem least special and wonderful that have the greatest impact.

The next time you are inconvenienced in some way, try being deliberate to give thanks. It may just change your outlook and make you feel richer in Christ.

Rejoice always; pray without ceasing; in everything give thanks; for this is God's will for you in Christ Jesus.
I THESSALONIANS 5:16–18 NASB

DECEMBER 4

"Family vacation." The words conjure up images of days at the lake, campfires with roasted marshmallows, and sleepy kids sharing rooms. Road trips full of car games and laughter, stops at quirky gas stations and just the right snacks. Sightseeing and creating memories—enough for a lifetime.

Often those sweet pictures in our head don't quite match up with the reality of a family trip. Vacations can be stressful, taking us out of well-developed routines and throwing us at the mercy of compromise. The kids may spend the trip bickering, overtired, and cranky.

But God asks us to give thanks and be joyful, and He means it—even when we're jammed together in the family minivan. With open hearts and an open road, let's share the love of Christ with all those whom we encounter, not forgetting to include our family among them.

And give thanks for everything to God the Father in the name of our Lord Jesus Christ.
EPHESIANS 5:20 NLT

DECEMBER 5

Our heavenly Father knows we get weary. He also knows when we need to be held and loved by Him until we're back to the point where we have the strength to love others. In our down times, we can look up and know He is everything we need. We can also know that He doesn't want us to be afraid (a side effect of weariness!), but that He wants us to know His power and love. So if you're weary right now, get settled in the lap of His love. Sit there quietly until your spirit gathers courage enough that you can go on—fearlessly!

God has not given us a spirit of fear, but of power and of love and of a sound mind.
II TIMOTHY 1:7 NKJV

DECEMBER 6

It's one of the strangest, most wonderful phenomena in life: loving. Love is made for giving. Hang onto what you have without sharing, and it will grow stagnant in you. You might begin to feel lonely, detached, unloved yourself. But give the love you have—and instead of feeling empty, you'll be filled right back up by the Lord.

He's just waiting for you to share it. You were made for it. And He loves filling your tank as soon as you have room!

God is love. So if you have God, you have an endless supply. The more generous you are with it, the more generous He will be with you!

Beloved, let us love one another, for love
is from God; and everyone who loves
is born of God and knows God.
I JOHN 4:7–8 NASB

DECEMBER 7

Being a mom is hard. It's easy to let the rough moments from the day replay over and over at night when the house is finally quiet. It's easy to believe that kids will only remember their mom being frustrated. What's hard is leaning into forgiveness. Truly believing in the depths of your heart that your transgressions have been removed—as far as the east is from the west. This is how the Father loves and forgives His children. Completely. Fully. Wholly. Without looking back. This is what it means to be forgiven, to be given compassion in mercy. This is how God encourages moms to continue forgiving their kids and themselves, day after day, moment by moment.

As far as the east is from the west, so far has He removed our transgressions from us. As a father has compassion on his children, so the Lord *has compassion on those who fear Him.*

PSALM 103:12–13 HCSB

DECEMBER 8

Imagine if your child were being accused of plagiarism in college. The professor and principal are prepared to suspend her based on circumstantial evidence. But you know that she worked all weekend to write the report in her own words! How easy would it be for you to stay quiet when injustice is being served?

We want justice, because our God is a just God. We've been wired to want what is right for ourselves and the ones we love. There's nothing wrong with that! But sometimes the very best policy is to stand back and watch the Lord work, instead of getting angry. He has a plan. And not always but sometimes we get in the way of what He wants to do.

[He] emptied Himself, taking the form of a bond-servant, and being made in the likeness of men. Being found in appearance as a man, He humbled Himself by becoming obedient to the point of death, even death on a cross.

PHILIPPIANS 2:7–8 NASB

DECEMBER 9

The judge stared down at the defendant, about to make his ruling. "You have admitted your guilt. I have no choice but to sentence you to life in prison." The defendant's father spoke out from the crowd, "Please, your honor! Let me take my son's place!"

"But you too are guilty of murder, sir. You cannot serve two sentences."

The courtroom door opened and a young man walked in. The judge's own son.

"Father, I know I am innocent. But I want to take this man's place. He is guilty. But I want to set him free."

The judge gasped. He was filled with sorrow and love at his own son's selflessness. "So be it," he said. "Young man, you are free to go."

He made Him who knew no sin to be sin on our behalf, so that we might become the righteousness of God in Him.
II CORINTHIANS 5:21 NASB

DECEMBER 10

Maybe the day isn't going so well. Everyone woke up on the wrong side of the bed, and everything continued downhill from there. And once the crabbiness invades, it's hard to take back the reins. But the good news is that no matter how terrible today has been, tomorrow is coming with all of its new mercy. God, in His great love, offers us a do-over each and every day. It's amazing! With the sun comes new compassion. Fresh mercy. A clean slate. Renewed grace. A chance to get up on the right side of the bed and keep that momentum going. Thank goodness for God's great love and for all that He blesses us with in each and every sunrise.

Because of the Lord's great love we are not consumed, for His compassions never fail. They are new every morning; great is Your faithfulness.
LAMENTATIONS 3:22–23 NIV

DECEMBER 11

Thunder rolls in the distance and your daughter darts down the steps to find you. "Mom? M–Mom?"

"Right here, sweetie. Right here."

Slipping her arms around your waist, she whispers, "Was that thunder?"

"Yes, but you don't need to be afraid. We are safe inside the house."

You've felt the same fear in your life. It wasn't over thunder but over trying circumstances or scary situations adults face. God is her refuge in the storm and He is yours too. He is ever faithful to protect both you and yours. What if you took a moment to remember to choose faith over fear?

He will cover you with His feathers, and under His wings you will find refuge; His faithfulness will be your shield and rampart.
PSALM 91:4 NIV

DECEMBER 12

There are no perfect words when praying to God, except the ones that are most genuine and sincere. But Jesus did give us a clue as to how to pray in power.

a. Our Father is glorious and holy; tell Him!
b. His kingdom is perfect; ask for its influence here on earth and in your circumstances.
c. God knows best; let Him lead.

Prayer is most powerful when you partner with God in the way He suggests. Partnership doesn't necessarily mean reading words on a page. It means using your heart, your voice, and your desire to bring His kingdom here today.

Pray, then, in this way: "Our Father who is in heaven, hallowed be Your name. Your kingdom come. Your will be done, on earth as it is in heaven."
MATTHEW 6:9–10 NASB

DECEMBER 13

Moms are the memory makers, the managers of the details, and the safe haven for their people. Sometimes amid the details and driving, the laundry and dishes, the tears and arguments, the diapers and homework…it's easy to let joy slip through the cracks. And when things are plain old hard, it's even easier to forget about joy altogether. That's when God calls us to lean into Him and to rely on His joy to make our hearts stronger.

Isn't it interesting that His joy becomes strength for His children? Joy makes us stronger. Joy strengthens relationships, brightens days, makes the mundane glorious. And God makes it available by the bucketload. So on the next hard day, or even the next ordinary one, count on the joy of the Lord to lighten your load—and your heart.

The joy of the Lord is your strength.
NEHEMIAH 8:10 NIV

DECEMBER 14

You, friend, are a smart person. You know many things. You've been given all sorts of knowledge and experience. But even the wisest and oldest among us is a mere blip on the screen of God's eternal plan. He is the Master Architect, with a view to everything. Before time began, for the last two thousand–plus years, and until a new heaven and a new earth take place.

Don't be offended or hurt if something doesn't make sense. There's a LOT you don't know, along with everyone else! God is working all things together for good…and that takes a lot of orchestration. Simply trusting Him and following His lead is the most peaceful, restful way to go.

Do all things without grumbling or disputing.
PHILIPPIANS 2:14 NASB

DECEMBER 15

This is your day. Right now. This moment. Whatever year you're reading this. At the time your clock currently reads. You can make a difference right now, for the person you're sitting next to. To the child who eats your cooking. To the girl who scans your groceries. To the stranger who just crossed in front of your car. You have this. very. allotted. second. to have an impact on the world. There's no point in waiting, because what if waiting means missing out on the opportunity to bless and be blessed?

A million such moments pass every day: your chance to change the world, one tiny little seed at a time.

As for the days of our life, they contain seventy years, or if due to strength, eighty years, yet their pride is but labor and sorrow; for soon it is gone and we fly away.

PSALM 90:10 NASB

DECEMBER 16

Try this experiment. Go out into public and just smile. A lot. At everyone. At the store, the coffee shop, the gym, on the street. Keep a tally of how many people smile back. It may amaze you!

Cheerfulness is contagious. And when you share cheer in the name of Jesus, He helps! You may find yourself growing more and more cheerful as you share the smiles you have. Because He comes along and fills your tank over and over again.

The Lord loves your willingness to give others what He has given you. And there's only good that comes from sharing a smile.

Bright eyes gladden the heart; good news puts fat on the bones.
PROVERBS 15:30 NASB

DECEMBER 17

Giving is such a beautiful reflection of God. No wonder it spreads such joy! Giving is love in action, and God calls—He commands—us to love. So write that note, make a call, open a door, tip generously…. Look for ways to give, and God will give you ways to do it!

Cheerful givers are the ones God prizes.
II CORINTHIANS 9:7 TLB

DECEMBER 18

The children of God are never alone. Sometimes it can feel lonely. Sometimes having people around becomes very important. But in the end, we have the Lord's presence at all times.

If you have Jesus, you have the Holy Spirit. You carry the kingdom of God with you wherever you go. That means you could be in the middle of a pagan country and still carry His light—which can never be extinguished!

Just try turning on a flashlight in a dark room. Does the darkness dampen the light? Or does the light illuminate the darkness?

You were made to shine, not cower. So go be bright with His love.

The Lord will guard your going out and your coming in from this time forth and forever.
PSALM 121:8 NASB

DECEMBER 19

The truth is, Jesus is enough. He is enough when you don't know what to do. He has the answers. Or when you're on the best vacation of your life, it is wonderful—but still less fulfilling than the fullness of Jesus. Measure everything by His standard: total acceptance, absolute joy, complete fulfillment, unending love. What could possibly compare to any of that alone, never mind all together?

Take the joy of Jesus with you, and it will keep the rest of life in perspective. His joy allows you to weather a storm, comfort a friend, and truly enjoy a celebration. When you have Jesus, you have all the confidence in the world to live in joy.

These things I have spoken to you so that My joy may be in you, and that your joy may be made full.
JOHN 15:11 NASB

DECEMBER 20

Jesus has a track record for enlisting the least prepared, least expected people. Not because He's a bad judge of character but because He's the best! He sees potential, adds the necessary training, and transforms the weak into ministers of His grace.

And it doesn't stop after boot camp! Jesus is into continuing education. He remains a mentor for life, leading His people through Holy Spirit courses on love, joy, peace, patience, kindness, goodness, faithfulness, gentleness, and self-control. It's a comprehensive program, designed to bring you to completion with Him one day. So if you're a student, you're in the very best hands. Take courage that Jesus believes in you!

Now as they observed the confidence of Peter and John and understood that they were uneducated and untrained men, they were amazed, and began to recognize them as having been with Jesus.

ACTS 4:13 NASB

DECEMBER 21

Today is an empty canvas. Paint it with moments that make God smile. When you were created, He put a unique combination of gifts in you. He knew exactly how you would color the world more beautifully. All that you are is a part of all that He is—and today is an opportunity to let it shine.

It is God Himself who has made us what we are.
EPHESIANS 2:10 TLB

DECEMBER 22

She looks down at her tight-laced skates, takes a deep breath, and steps out onto the rink. Whoops! Slippery! This is going to be an adventure! She wobbles along, holding tightly to the wall for a while. She is thankful for knee and elbow pads.

As she starts to go down for yet another tumble, she feels a hand reach under her arm. Mommy! The mother holds her up, then grabs her hand tightly. Together they skate along—mother on steady feet and daughter on wobbly legs. But her confidence is already soaring in her mother's firm grip.

If you stay connected to God, He will not let your foot slip. It takes two to hold hands…so if you grip Him, He promises to grip you back.

Now to Him who is able to keep you from stumbling, and to make you stand in the presence of His glory blameless with great joy, to the only God our Savior, through Jesus Christ our Lord, be glory, majesty, dominion and authority, before all time and now and forever. Amen.

JUDE 24–25 NASB

DECEMBER 23

Emotions are a gift from the Lord! Even Jesus wept with sorrow, felt anger, and sang in happiness. Emotions are a great signal for what's going on inside of you and should be paid attention to.

Emotions are always most effective when they are surrendered and submitted to God. After all, as the Creator of both our emotions and our means of feeling and expressing them, He knows best what to do with them! Allow Him to lead you through your emotions, and at the right times you will be able to respond in love and confidence to others. Allow your emotions to control you, and you may find yourself saying or doing things you regret later.

A gentle answer turns away wrath,
but a harsh word stirs up anger.
PROVERBS 15:1 NASB

DECEMBER 24

Before a child learns to temper her imagination, she can think up impossible storylines with the least likely adventures, with the most amazing gusto. Where else are you likely to hear of the purple penguin who befriends a spotted buffalo as they search for rainbow tokens worth special candy prizes in the lightning bug forest?

But even as wild as a child's imagination can be, the plans of God are even more unfathomable. We see dim glimpses through the Word: seas of glass, streets of gold, angels like many-eyed beings...but God's dreams and plans for us will never be seen this side of heaven. So for now, dream huge. Keep dreaming. And watch as He overwhelms you with even more.

Now to Him who is able to do far more abundantly beyond all that we ask or think, according to the power that works within us, to Him be the glory.

EPHESIANS 3:20–21 NASB

DECEMBER 25

There will come a day when comparison is a thing of the past. No more "keeping up with the Joneses." No more competition between neighbors and friends—unless it's just a fun game of ping pong (if that exists in heaven)! Girls won't feel pressured to dress in the latest fashions. Boys won't try to show off with their latest skateboarding tricks. Or if they do, the oohs and ahhs will come from people who are genuinely impressed!

The kingdom of heaven is full of those who rejoice with those who rejoice. Practicing it then will be an everyday occurrence. Practicing it now will make you a hot commodity!

We are your reason to be proud as you also are ours, in the day of our Lord Jesus.
II CORINTHIANS 1:14 NASB

DECEMBER 26

Your friend shows up to lunch after a vacation overseas. You notice she has a fancy new handbag. "I got it for such an incredible price, only twenty dollars! It would cost two hundred here!" As you admire the bag, you glance again at the name brand. You squint…and see that the famous label is misspelled. You've spotted an impostor.

The true things of God don't have to try and convince anyone of their goodness. The closer you scrutinize, the more integrity you see in His handiwork. Not so with impostors, who have to hide blemishes. The Lord doesn't mind close examination. In fact, He welcomes it.

Beware of the false prophets, who come to you in sheep's clothing, but inwardly are ravenous wolves. You will know them by their fruits.
MATTHEW 7:15–16 NASB

DECEMBER 27

There is one thing that all mothers will agree on. Parenting is exhausting and relentless in its everyday demands. No mother on the planet will argue that what she does on a daily basis doesn't take every last ounce of human effort. Yes, some days are easier than others. But oh, the hard days when bedtime can't come quickly enough…after a stressful day at work, after a long night of nursing a colicky newborn, after a long day of entertaining energetic toddlers, after coming home from the emergency room with a sick child, after waiting up for your daughter to come home from a date, after watching your son pull out of the driveway alone for the first time. Parenting doesn't care how tired you are, but God does. The source of all refreshment is calling your name. Schedule time for Him, and receive the rest He promises.

Then Jesus said, "Come to Me, all of you who are weary and carry heavy burdens, and I will give you rest."
MATTHEW 11:28 NLT

DECEMBER 28

God puts the light of His love within us while the world puts a spotlight on what we do. When we trust God to guide us, we allow His love to govern us and the more often love becomes a part of all we do. Leading a selfless and considerate life doesn't come by chance, though. It comes when we choose love!

Let everyone see that you are unselfish
and considerate in all you do.
PHILIPPIANS 4:5 TLB

DECEMBER 29

Moms know dirty hands. They can spot dirt under the fingernails a mile away. But, can we spot the stain of sin on ourselves as quickly? Is our spiritual radar tuned to the sin that so easily entangles us? Sometimes it is not so easy to spot sin. We get used to it and even rely on it. We like our selfishness, our pride, our self-pity, and even our whininess and complaining. (We know kids that have those on lockdown!) The good news is that God gives us a simple way of washing the sin from our hands and hearts. In fact, He did it for us when He sent Jesus to die on the cross for our sins. Just as our kids only have to turn on the sink and pick up the soap, we only have to look to Jesus and He willingly washes it away for us!

Who may ascend the mountain of the Lord? Who may stand in His holy place? The one who has clean hands and a pure heart, who does not trust in an idol or swear by a false god.

PSALM 24:3–4 NIV

DECEMBER 30

At a young age, a child learns to squeeze his eyes tight and clasp his hands together at the table when it's time to pray. Most likely he learns because his parents begin showing him that classic posture of prayer when they want him to learn that praying is important. Most adults don't squeeze their eyes shut and their hands together when they speak with God. Why? Because they know that prayer is deeper than hand motions; it is a heart-to-heart conversation. What we look like when we pray doesn't matter, really.

There's a lot we learn in the beginning that serves to get us started, but we make adjustments as we internalize the true meanings behind our actions. What God cares about is the inside—not the looks.

Whether, then, you eat or drink or whatever you do, do all to the glory of God.
I CORINTHIANS 10:31 NASB

DECEMBER 31

They've been married for forty-six years. They know each other well—all the qualities and all the quirks. She knows his likes and dislikes. So when she speaks for both of them, she does so with a desire to honor the kind of man he is. She would never, for example, commit him to a dance-off at the local charity event! Likewise, he knows her. He likes to cook. But he would never commit her to cooking for one of his work events. Cooking is not her thing.

Love means caring very much to respect who the other person is. The Lord, in His amazing love, does this for us. And when we love Him well, we are acting on His behalf with that same kind of deference.

Let the words of my mouth and the meditation
of my heart be acceptable in Your sight,
O Lord, my rock and my Redeemer.
PSALM 19:14 NASB

Dear Friend,

This book was prayerfully crafted with you, the reader, in mind—every word, every sentence, every page—was thoughtfully written, designed, and packaged to encourage you . . . right where you are this very moment. At DaySpring, our vision is to see every person experience the life-changing message of God's love. So, as we worked through rough drafts, design changes, edits, and details, we prayed for you to deeply experience His unfailing love, indescribable peace, and pure joy. It is our sincere hope that through these Truth-filled pages your heart will be blessed, knowing that God cares about you—your desires and disappointments, your challenges and dreams.

He knows. He cares. He loves you unconditionally.

BLESSINGS!
THE DAYSPRING BOOK TEAM

Acknowledgments

Special thanks to the lovely moms who helped write this book.

Paige DeRuyscher · Kristin Morris · Anna Rendell · Amanda White · Rachel Wojo

Thank you for writing from your hearts to encourage other mothers—mothers who will be blessed by your willingness to be open and honest about the ups and downs of motherhood.